About the Silver Screen Cities books

The books in the Silver Screen Cities series are a celebration of city cinema-going. Written by a filmgoing flâneur who loves wandering around cities as much as he enjoys sitting in cinemas watching films, the Silver Screen Cities books spring from the notion that visiting cinemas and their neighbourhoods is a great way of getting to know different cities.

An eclectic mix of films are covered in the books. A mainstream Hollywood blockbuster in one chapter may be followed by an obscure black and white arthouse film in the next.

Unlike conventional collections of film reviews, the Silver Screen Cities books are about the whole experience surrounding cinema-going, rather than just a series of reviews. The film reviews sometimes take up only one or two paragraphs in a chapter, because city cinema-going is about much more than just the film that is being shown – it's also about the cinema itself and the audience watching the film; the unique character and atmosphere of different cities with their bars, cafés, restaurants, and art museums; and the feeling of freedom that comes from wandering a city's streets before or after seeing a film.

Also by David Kintore

Silver Screen Cities Amsterdam & Brussels
Silver Screen Cities Lisbon (forthcoming)

SILVER SCREEN CITIES

Celebrating city cinema-going

Tokyo & London

DAVID KINTORE

Silver Screen Cities Publications

Published by Silver Screen Cities Publications 2014

ISBN 978-90-822393-0-0

Silver Screen Cities™ is a trademark of Silver Screen Cities Publications.

Silver Screen Cities Publications
The Hague, The Netherlands
www.silverscreencities.com

Cover Design by James, GoOnWrite.com
Text design and ebook by Ebookconverting.com

Contents

TOKYO

LONDON

TOKYO

The Imaginarium of Doctor Parnassus

Toho Cinema Yurakuza

Winter days are mild in Tokyo, though the evening chill sets in quickly as soon as darkness falls. So this cold February evening I don't linger as I walk past Kamiyacho and Toranomon on my way to Yurakucho, in the centre of Tokyo, where Toho Cinema Yurakuza is located.

With its unusual lattice exterior, the looming Peninsula Hotel is a useful landmark in this part of the city. From here the lights of Marunouchi can be seen reflected in the waters of the moat surrounding the Imperial Palace. At a warmer time of year I would stop to enjoy the view. But tonight I head straight on to the cinema, where *The Imaginarium of Doctor Parnassus* is playing.

Toho Cinema Yurakuza is a wonderful place. Luxurious thick red curtains are draped along the auditorium walls, the seats are very comfortable, and even a visit to the toilets is an aesthetically pleasing experience: they are the most spotlessly clean I have ever seen, and painted a vivid turquoise topped with shiny glitter.

Back in the auditorium, with this being Tokyo, the first advert shown is for earthquake-resistant domestic appliances. The trailers that follow the adverts include one for a film that is due to open in a couple of months time, called *My Darling is a Foreigner*. It's about a cross-cultural couple, a Japanese woman and a Western man. The story is one that Western male expatriates and Japanese women can obviously relate to. But on the evidence of this trailer I won't be in any hurry to check out the film; it looks twee and the actor playing the Western male looks very annoying.

The trailers finish and it's onto tonight's film, *The Imaginarium of Doctor Parnassus*. The film is directed by Terry Gilliam, who brags in the official trailer about how marvellous his film is. Gilliam seems enraptured by his own febrile imagination. Unfortunately, this doesn't translate into a particularly engaging film.

The film is a curate's egg. Visually, it is stunning. The music is suitably hyperbolic. And some of the acting is very good, particularly by Tom Waits as the devil and by Christopher Plummer, who is superb as Doctor Parnassus. The problem, though, is the script, which is feeble. The dialogue constantly falls flat. Verne Troyer does what he can with a string of lame punchlines. It's not his fault they do not come off; he is just given little to work with.

Hopefully director Gilliam's next film will have a better script. By the time this film ends I'm left with a feeling of what might have been. The film is spectacular and it has an excellent cast, but the whole thing is let down by the dialogue. It takes some kind of perverse talent to have at your disposal not just one heart-throb but several: Johnny Depp, Colin Farrell, Jude Law, and the late Heath Ledger, and yet still turn out a film that falls flat.

With a sense of disappointment, I head out of the cinema after the film ends.

It's a Monday night, so the town is fairly downbeat. But there is still a bit of urban bustle around the Yurakucho train tracks. On one street corner a young salaryman is slumped comatose next to his briefcase. Apart from that, there is not much inebriation to be seen.

One of the great things about living in Tokyo is the lack of street crime. The unconscious salaryman will almost certainly wake up to find his briefcase still there beside him, not stolen as it would be in most cities in other countries.

Did You Hear About the Morgans?

Shinagawa Prince Cinema

Not many tourists make it down to Shinagawa in south Tokyo. It may be off the beaten track for time-pressed visitors, but for locals and resident expatriates Shinagawa's charms include the urban bustle around its train station, a more down-to-earth vibe than you find in the centre of Tokyo, and its proximity to the romantic waterfront of Tennozu Isle.

It's a fresh and breezy mid-March afternoon as I walk down Daiichi Keihin to Shinagawa Prince Cinema, the venue for today's film, *Did You Hear About The Morgans?*

The cinema is located in a shopping mall, which doesn't appeal much to me. But there are plenty of tempting restaurants in the vicinity to make a cinema trip to this neck of the woods worthwhile.

Shinagawa station has a constellation of eating places of all kinds, from cheap and cheerful ramen bars down by the train tracks to upscale fine dining in more sophisticated surroundings. Approximately one minute's walk from the cinema entrance stands a quirky circular bar restaurant named Shusaron, which specializes in vintage saké and looks well worth a visit.

But today all I have time for before the film is to grab a 600-yen draft beer from the cinema snack counter. Armed with this beverage I enter Cinema 3 and locate my seat. At this point, fifteen minutes before the showing is due to start, I am the only person in the auditorium.

Cinema 3 has a decent-sized screen. After the mildly frustrating experience of being penned in my mid-row seat at Toho Cinema Yurakuza a few days ago by unmoving cinema-goers on either side of me as the credits rolled interminably at the end of *The Imaginarium of Dr Parnassus*, I make sure today that I have a better seat for effecting a reasonably swift exit. Seat G3 is perfect: at the end of a row, mid-way back from the screen.

Hugh Grant was in town a few days ago to promote *Did You Hear About The Morgans?* At the Tokyo press conference he said that Japanese women have always been amongst his biggest fans.

When I mention that I am going to see *Did You Hear About the Morgans?* today, I am told – by one Japanese woman – "You will be the only man in the audience". Although the prospect of being the only representative of the male of the species is slightly daunting, I go ahead anyway and buy a ticket for the film. As it turns out, two other males show up for the screening so although we are vastly outnumbered, I am not the freakish solitary rogue male in the audience that had been predicted.

Hugh Grant and Sarah Jessica Parker may be an unlikely combination, but in this enjoyable film there is good chemistry between them.

Sarah Jessica Parker's character is a jittery Manhattanite, focused on her career and driven by ambition. She seems to be successful, glamorous, dazzling. So far, so *Sex and the City*. But in this film there is a warmth and a tenderness to her character that doesn't come through in her role in the TV series. Here she gives a subtle performance of understated yet deep pain at the infidelity she has suffered at the hands of Grant's character. There are no histrionics from her, just a weary and profound disappointment that she has been let down by someone she once trusted.

Grant, on the other hand, does a good job in mixing the exuberance of trying to win Parker back with the frustration of not knowing how often he needs to apologize for his one transgression.

The soundtrack brims with good country music and 1970s southern rock. There is a wonderful panoramic shot of Grant and Parker's characters jogging across a huge open plain with an endless sky above, whilst Hank Williams sings 'Why Don't You Love Me'. This is a big part of the film's appeal: the surreal presence of quintessential English fop Hugh Grant in what is to him a completely alien world of country music, western movie landscapes, and diehard Republican heartland America.

As well as Hank Williams, the soundtrack also features current country king George Strait and southern rock legends The Allman Brothers Band. The music is a perfect backdrop to the main characters' forced retreat to a slower rural lifestyle away from frenetic New York City.

Sam Elliott and Mary Steenburgen are both very good as the couple who accommodate Grant and Parker during their stay in their rural backwater. There probably won't ever be a sequel made to this film, but if there is, it will be interesting to see the relationship between the two couples developed a bit further.

This film has not received many rave reviews, but for fans of romantic comedies it delivers what it promises. Anyone who likes Hugh Grant or Sarah Jessica Parker should enjoy it; it's not a classic by any means, but as a date movie it's not bad at all.

Leaving the cinema, I turn right towards Shinagawa station where the early evening commuters are hurrying homeward. A left turn rather than a right turn would lead towards Sempo Hospital, where I had to go last month for the annual health check that is provided for all employees by their companies in Japan.

This annual health check is quite an experience. At my most recent health check, I was given an unusual instruction.

"Do not belch please. Do not belch please."

This was the first time I had ever been asked not to belch. The person issuing the preemptive command not to belch was a doctor at Sempo Hospital. This particular part of the health check was a stomach x-ray. The doctor gives me baking-soda crystals to swallow and a cup full of milky barium which apparently allows clearer imaging of my insides when the x-ray takes place. The crystals have a gassy effect when you swallow them, which can lead to the belching which the doctor was keen to avoid.

After I have swallowed the milky liquid, things get a bit alarming. I am told to stand on a machine that tilts and swivels while I hang on for dear life. I lie on my back and on my stomach and on my side as the doctor, who by now has retreated to the safety of his glass-fronted control room, operates the machine.

Over a speaker system he tells me to turn to the left, to the right, and all the way round. It must be an entertaining spectacle to watch from the sidelines, and the bizarreness of the experience makes it the highlight of the health check for me; it's much more memorable than the chest x-ray, blood test, eyesight test, and so on.

When it's all over, I am given some laxatives to take later in the day to make sure that the barium gets flushed out my system pronto.

Tonight, though, there is no need to sprint home to be in the reassuring vicinity of a toilet. Instead, I saunter out the cinema, stroll past the elegant white-washed edifice of the Singapore Seafood Republic restaurant, and head on down to the main road where the large rectangular box of Shinagawa station stands off to the right with its unusual arches-and-pipes facade. It's good to have a walk and stretch the legs after sitting in a cinema for a couple of hours.

Back home at my apartment in Azabudai an hour later, I crack open a bottle of saké.

When I first came to Japan, all sakés tasted pretty much the same to my uneducated palate. Given the huge number of saké brands that are available here, I decided to do a bit of research on the topic so that I would be able to appreciate the drink more.

It turns out that there are four basic tasting terms that are used to describe saké. There are actually a lot more than four, but it becomes highly confusing if you try to get your head round all the different ways of evaluating saké. Time is better spent drinking the stuff than analyzing it, so I just stick to the basic four terms: *kaori*, which is the fragrance; *kuchiatari*, which is the impact the saké makes as an initial impression in your mouth; *fukurami*, which describes how the saké feels as it spreads inside your mouth; and finally, *kire*, which is the tail, namely, does the flavour of the saké disappear instantly after you swallow it or does it linger.

By using these terms and by committing to a rigorous ongoing programme of saké sampling, I can now appreciate much more the subtle and not so subtle differences between different types of saké. Another good way for the dedicated saké student to learn how to appreciate the different styles is to order the tasting sets that are often available in restaurants. These sets typically include four or five small servings of different sakés. By tasting them one after another in quick succession, you begin to notice the differences in kaori, kuchiatari, fukurami, and kire.

The saké I have tonight is a wonderful one called Yamagata-Masamune. It's from Yamagata Prefecture in the Tohoku region of Japan. According to my scribbled tasting notes, the kaori of this brew is light and grassy; the kuchiatari is smooth and tastes of pears; in terms of fukurami, it doesn't rush around the mouth, and it has a strong but elegant flavour; and the kire is clean and quick. I give it a 'five star plus' rating, the highest available in my burgeoning saké tasting chart.

What a superb drink. And the great thing is, there are hundreds more sakés out there just waiting to be discovered.

Sherlock Holmes

Marunouchi Louvre Cinema

What, no fog? As a diehard fan of the classic black and white Sherlock Holmes films in which Basil Rathbone plays the hero, I had been looking forward to thick mysterious fog shrouding the London street scenes in this new version of *Sherlock Holmes* directed by Guy Ritchie and starring Robert Downey Jr in the title role. So it's disheartening to view the opening scene unfurl through streets that are devoid of fog. But this is a fleeting disappointment, soon dispelled.

I approached this film with mixed feelings. How could it ever live up to the elegant perfection of the Basil Rathbone films? Would this be a dumbed-down Hollywood abomination, unworthy of the Sherlock Holmes name? On the other hand, Robert Downey Jr is a superb actor and if any current actor could potentially nail the Sherlock Holmes character, he would get my vote as the most likely to succeed.

And succeed he does. The film is wonderful.

Of course, there will always be some fans who will bemoan any attempt to render Sherlock Holmes in a way that is different to what has gone before. The makers of this new version do give a different spin to some elements of the Sherlock Holmes character; but it's more a matter of emphasizing what was always there in the original Holmes stories, rather than brazenly playing around with the legend. The violence is more brutal than it is in the old Basil Rathbone films, but you can't really argue with that – the violence was always there in the books, it's just that in the old days, cinema did not portray violence as graphically as it does today.

What is most impressive about this new version, particularly to people like me for whom Basil Rathbone will always be the ultimate Holmes, is that Robert Downey Jr as Holmes and Jude Law as his sidekick Watson are incredibly faithful to the spirit of the original stories. Gone may be the buffoonery of Watson as played by Nigel Bruce in the old Rathbone films. In its place is a Watson who is still very much the junior partner in the relationship with Holmes. But in the Jude Law incarnation, Watson acquires an individuality and shrewdness that the Nigel Bruce incarnation did not possess.

Nigel Bruce was great as the lovable yet constantly bewildered Watson. Jude Law, though, injects extra energy into the Watson character without sacrificing the all important dynamic between him and Holmes. The petty squabbling between Robert Downey Jr and Jude Law over the experiments that Holmes has been conducting on the pet dog is very funny. The rapport between the two actors is marvellous. They really have captured the spirit of the original characters.

A good, solid supporting cast play familiar figures such as Inspector Lestrade and housekeeper Mrs Hudson. The villain of the piece is played powerfully by Mark Strong as Lord Blackwood, a character who is Moriarty in all but name.

Visually the film is very striking, particularly in its dramatic stylized night skies over London as seen from the River Thames.

The film has a sharp edge, tinged with madness. The soundtrack is fantastic; Hans Zimmer is at the top of his game, his music as much a character in this film as any of the people in it. And the use of Irish folk music in some scenes is a surprising choice, but it works brilliantly. The deep rumbling groove of 'The Rocky Road to Dublin' by the Dubliners fits the mood of the film perfectly.

When the film ends, I come out of the cinema hoping that they will go on to make a sequel, either an original story or based on one of Arthur Conan Doyle's stories. I still want to see some fog, though.

The cinema in which the film is showing is a wonderful majestic place, although slightly tricky to find. The box office is out on the street by an awning that says 'Yurakucho Mullion' rather than next to the cinema itself, which you access by going into the adjacent shopping mall. It's best to leave yourself some time before the film is due to start, to make sure that you can actually find the cinema.

Before the film I had time for a quick Moretti beer at Barissimo, an Italian bar on the opposite side of the street from the box office. After the film finishes I head to the nearby Udon & Jizake restaurant for a very good meal of salad, tuna, fried chicken, and udon noodles with a bit of ginger, all washed down with a couple of sakés: Nara Spring Deer, a very dry junmai, and the excellent Drunken Whale from Kochi, a junmai ginjo.

The term *junmai* refers to pure rice saké that has not had any distilled alcohol added to it. Junmai tends to be bold and flavourful, sometimes too much so. I often prefer *honjozo*, which is a type of premium saké just like junmai, but honjozo comes with a small amount of alcohol added to it. This creates a lighter and more subtle flavour that is very refreshing and drinkable.

As for the term *ginjo*, that is a quality classification applied to saké which has had a certain percentage of the rice grains polished away before the brewing process begins. At the top of the saké quality tree stands *daiginjo*, which refers to those sakés that have had the highest percentage of the original rice grains polished away prior to brewing.

After the meal I walk back alongside the Yurakucho train tracks. The salaryman restaurants are brimming with office workers no doubt discussing the recent bombshell that just hit the sumo world – the sudden retirement of sumo champion Asashoryu.

In the last couple of years, the sumo world has been dominated by two *yokozuna* (grand champions),

Asashoryu and Hakuho, both of whom are from Mongolia. They have completely different styles and are perfectly matched. Hakuho is the clean-cut good guy, a family man, always dignified. Asashoryu is the colourful rebel, unconstrained by sumo's solemn etiquette. Neither man is huge, unlike the famous 'Dump Truck' fighter from a few years back. Instead, Hakuho and Asashoryu are both very fast, very powerful and just too quick-thinking for their opponents.

When I first came to Japan and started watching sumo on NHK's live coverage of the tournaments, I couldn't see much difference between the wrestlers.

I didn't know my Asashoryu from my Kotoshu.

But soon I started to appreciate the skill, power and technique of the two yokozuna. For a while I was a neutral, preferring neither Asashoryu nor Hakuho over the other. But gradually I found myself rooting for Asashoryu because he is such an exciting wrestler to watch. He is completely unpredictable. He might demolish an opponent within seconds or he might toil laboriously to finish off an opponent whom the more predictably efficient Hakuho would have dispatched much quicker.

But when Asashoryu is on form he is riveting to watch. He fires up the crowd, too. Even those who prefer Hakuho get caught up in Asashoryu's pre-bout ritual, which culminates in a savage thumping of his own chest that intimidates his opponent and electrifies the crowd.

One of Asashoryu's finest moments was on the final day of the September 2009 Grand Tournament at Tokyo's Ryogoku Kokugikan. Going into the final day, Asashoryu was unbeaten whilst Hakuho had lost one fight.

When the two of them face off on the final day, Hakuho launches an unstoppable charge that knocks Asashoryu backwards. Hakuho quickly throws Asashoryu down.

A play-off follows to decide who will be tournament champion.

Backstage during the break between the initial fight and the play-off, Hakuho looks cool and calm and in control. Asashoryu is slumped on a bench, looking like a beaten man. But when the wrestlers re-enter the ring for the play-off, Asashoryu draws on all his character and fighting spirit. He performs his pre-bout ritual with his usual fervour.

If you are going to have any chance of beating the near flawless Hakuho, you have to get off to a great start, and this time Asashoryu does. He forces Hakuho off-balance straightaway and turns the fight into the fluid fast-moving spectacle that he excels at, rather than the static style of bout that Hakuho prefers.

The crowd senses that something special is happening and roars the fighters on. I am glued to the television screen in my Azabudai apartment, shouting for Asashoryu. The tv commentator's voice grows louder and more frenzied. Amid this uproar the two great yokozuna battle each other until, with a final flourish, Asashoryu sends Hakuho sprawling to the ground to claim the tournament in the most dramatic fashion imaginable. It is an epic performance by Asashoryu, who looked dead and buried in the interval between the first fight and the play-off. He was a magnificent champion.

Surprisingly, when Asashoryu announces his premature retirement due to an alleged drunken incident, the person who seems most upset about it is Hakuho. In a televised interview just after Asashoryu's retirement announcement, Hakuho is absolutely distraught, clearly very upset that his arch-rival has suddenly quit the scene. Hakuho is so choked up during the interview that he can hardly speak. He says how much he admires Asashoryu and how Asashoryu has been an inspiration to him.

Hakuho looks bereft and abandoned. To see such a big strong fighter so affected is very moving. With Asashoryu gone, Hakuho is now the only wrestler at yokozuna level, which is a considerable responsibility to carry.

The great rivalry between Hakuho and Asashoryu is now over. The sumo world will be a lot duller without Asashoryu in it.

Invictus

Shibuya Cine Palace

Shibuya Crossing is one of Tokyo's iconic sights. It is the famous intersection where huge crowds of pedestrians amass patiently on each point of the intersection, waiting to cross.

At its busiest times the crowds are like opposing armies awaiting the signal to charge.

When the moment comes, though, the crowds somehow manage to stream through each other remarkably smoothly. It might look like that a gigantic human gridlock is inevitable, but it never happens. The location appears in one scene of *Lost In Translation*; the film makers did their filming of it from a café that overlooks the bustling crossing.

Having navigated Shibuya Crossing, I find the cinema for today's film just a few minutes walk away.

Shibuya Cine Palace occupies the sixth and seventh floors of a nondescript building on a Shibuya backstreet. The ticket counter is on the seventh floor, whilst the screens are on the sixth floor. As the elevator does not stop on the sixth floor, patrons have to ride up to the seventh floor and then walk down one floor if they have already bought their tickets.

With an hour to spare before the showing, there is time to nip out to a nearby shopping mall for tea and scones at the refined Earl Tea Salon.

Tonight's film, *Invictus*, is showing in Cinema 2. It's a mid-sized auditorium with comfortable seats and plenty leg room for tall gaijins like me. Into my cup-holder I place my bottle of Asahi Super Dry, not a brand I would normally choose but it is the only beer that the cinema stocks. Super Dry is the Asahi company's blockbuster beer brand. Like its mass-market American counterparts, its success is built on easy drinkability and relentless advertising.

Fortunately for beer aficionados, Japan now has a healthy number of craft breweries producing much more interesting brews. Komagatake Brewery's Minamishinsyu Beer, dry and tangy with notes of pine and heather; Kamakura Beer Brewing Company's Enoshima Beer; and Ibaraki-based Kiuchi Brewery's superb Hitachino Nest Beer all come to mind in this respect. There is also Ryujin Beer's Ozeno Yukidoke, a nice fruity beer in a stubby 330 ml bottle. For me, one bottle at a time is enough for Ozeno Yukidoke, I wouldn't quaff it as a session beer.

But here at the cinema tonight, Super Dry will have to do.

Invictus is several weeks into its Tokyo run. So the cinema is not full tonight, although it's still a healthy turnout. As rugby is not yet a mainstream sport here in Japan, it's likely that most of the audience have come because of Morgan Freeman and Matt Damon rather than to relive the 1995 Rugby World Cup on which the film is based.

A wry chuckle ripples through the audience in the scene where Morgan Freeman as Nelson Mandela is told about the awesome string of victories that the rampant New Zealand All Blacks have racked up on their way to the final of the tournament, notably the All Blacks demolition of Japan by a record 145-17 points.

Morgan Freeman is as close to perfect as any actor could be in the role of Nelson Mandela. Freeman exudes the dignity and charisma of Mandela, whilst also occasionally showing the chinks in Mandela's emotional armour.

The other hero of this improbable but true tale is François Pienaar, the captain of the South African Springboks rugby team, ably played by Matt Damon. The way in which the paths of Mandela and Pienaar cross reflects the reconciliation of South Africa's diverse society following the abolition of the apartheid system that had blighted the country for so long. Both men prove themselves to be true leaders through their willingness to face down elements within their own ranks who are reluctant to embrace the newly born Rainbow Nation.

Unusually for a sports film, the sporting action is actually pretty good and realistic. For rugby fans it's great to see a few original clips from the 1995 tournament, especially those featuring the All Blacks legendary powerhouse Jonah Lomu in his unstoppable, bone-crushing prime. The music in the soundtrack is wonderful. And director Clint Eastwood does a great job in keeping the plot focused when it could easily have got sidetracked by potential subplots reflecting the countless upheavals then occurring within South Africa.

Invictus is a great tribute to Mandela, Pienaar and everyone else who played their part in healing the wounds of South Africa during the early days of that reborn nation. Tonight's audience seems to be happy as the film ends.

It feels good to exit the cinema and plunge back into the vibrant sexy urban pulse of Shibuya.

The Hurt Locker

Shibuto Cine Tower

In the cold light of day, Tokyo can seem grey and sterile. But at night and in the early evening, when the light fades from the sky, Tokyo is magical. The neon buildings begin to shine as the sky turns from pale blue to deep blue to black. You get that in any city but here in Tokyo it is somehow different, more beautiful and more seductive.

In Tokyo, even busy city streets can be incredibly quiet. Walking along these busy but quiet streets feels like luxuriating in a cocoon, or a warm bath. Then, almost imperceptibly, the atmosphere livens up and gets boisterous as you reach one of the city's hubs. Tonight it is Shibuya. Even though it is just a Monday night, the street life is absolutely buzzing. There is good-humoured excited chatter all around.

It's invigorating to be immersed in Shibuya's happy swarm of humanity.

A useful landmark for finding tonight's cinema, Shibuto Cine Tower, is the cylindrical tower of Shibuya 109 on the other side of the road from the cinema. Shibuto Cine Tower has four screens, each located on a different floor of the building. *The Hurt Locker* is showing in the basement screen, which is decked out in mauve seating, mauve carpets, and mauve walls. Not particularly inspiring but not unpleasant either.

I get here twenty minutes before the showing is due to start. I manage to get an end of the row seat near the back of the auditorium to facilitate a sharp exit should that be required if the film is lousy and I need to walk out before the end.

It is not exactly 'stadium seating' in this auditorium. There is a very gentle slope from the back of the room down towards the screen, as you would expect. But then, in a baffling piece of design, the three rows of seats nearest the screen slope gently up rather than down. This would be annoying if you were sitting behind someone thus elevated above you and blocking your view.

The Hurt Locker lives up to its Oscar-winning hype. It's a great film, gripping and intense, with terrific performances by Jeremy Renner, Anthony Mackie and Brian Geraghty in the lead roles.

The best thing about *The Hurt Locker* is the masterful pacing of the film. Although it is a war film, the action scenes are balanced with extended sequences where there are no explosions or exchanges of gunfire. These spells of inaction are as compelling as the more 'dramatic' scenes, in that they establish the atmosphere of the Iraq location and give breathing space both to the actors and to the audience.

Sound, or the lack of it, is used very skilfully. We are not bludgeoned by non-stop action. Instead, the soundtrack often pulls back to nothing but sporadic ambient sound. This draws you in, rather than pinning you back in your seat.

Jeremy Renner is very good as Sergeant First Class William James, the reckless but inspiring leader of the bomb disposal unit whose existence in Baghdad and beyond is one of grim horror. But in this film there is no sermonizing about the horrors of war, and no political agenda is peddled. The film makers can take this non-partisan approach now that the war in Iraq is no longer constant front page news. Even just a couple of years ago it would have been difficult to justify such a seemingly objective take on the Iraq war; there would have been huge pressure to take a stand one way or the other regarding the war, either for or against.

But *The Hurt Locker* doesn't try to score any political points. It shows the gruesome nature of life in wartime Iraq but leaves the audience to reach their own judgement regarding the justification or foolishness of the Iraq war.

Anthony Mackie as Sergeant Sanborn and Brian Geraghty as Specialist Owen Eldridge put in excellent performances too. Mackie and Renner's characters have a good scene near the end, in which Mackie asks Renner how he can take such risks with his life when he has a wife and a kid back home. This scene is not forced at all, it is quiet and reflective and a good example of how the film blends action and characterization.

Although the film overall is well worthy of its awards and praise, the ending is executed very clumsily. The jump from Iraq back to the Renner character's wife and kid back home is done so suddenly that it feels like a different film. The mesmerizing quality of what has gone before is tossed away by this abrupt switch to domestic life. Unfortunately the film's spell is broken exactly when it should have been reaching its peak, and when the credits roll it is with a sense of anti-climax.

But all in all, there are very few off notes in this brilliant film.

Up in the Air

Toho Cinema Chanter

IT's mid-afternoon, late April. The morning's torrential rain has stopped and given way to a mild steaminess. It's a good time to be walking along the top of the embankment next to the wide moat that encircles the Imperial Palace. The grass, bushes and flowers are vividly coloured and have that invigorating after-the-rain freshness and fragrance.

From up by the British Embassy I walk downhill and south, enjoying the great view of the moat and palace grounds to the left and the tall office blocks of Marunouchi rising up ahead. Tokyo is looking beautiful today.

When I get down to Hibiya Park, a couple of American tourists ask me the way to Ginza. So I walk with them as far as the Peninsula Hotel and point them in the right direction, under the train tracks and straight on. I then head across to Toho Cinema Chanter to get a ticket for *Up in the Air*, George Clooney's film in which he plays a corporate axeman whose job is to tell company employees that they have been fired.

Because today is a Wednesday, I am surrounded by an audience that is overwhelmingly female. On Wednesdays there is a discount for women, who can get in for 1000 yen whereas we guys pay the usual 1800 yen. The discount, and the fact that this is a George Clooney movie, accounts for the unusually high ratio of females to males here tonight.

After you buy your ticket at the ground-floor ticket office, you need to take the lift to whichever floor your film is showing on. There are three screens. Very helpfully, inside the lift the buttons for each floor show not only the number of the floor but also the name of the film that is showing at the screen on that particular floor. So you don't need to worry about ending up on the wrong floor, you just press the button with your film's name on it.

Up in the Air has been on in Tokyo for a few weeks now, so it has been relegated to Screen 3.

Emerging from the lift, down in the basement, I go to the snack counter. I'm appalled to discover that they don't serve beer. Still, having just wolfed down a pizza with a beer in a nearby cheap Italian joint, I'm not too distraught. If I had arrived here gasping for a beer, my mood would not have been so benign.

The trailers start as soon as I get to the Screen 3 auditorium, and I don't have to look at the dull decor for long. One of the trailers is dreadful. It is for what looks like a dismal teen flick titled *Roller Girls Diary*, although that title might be just for the Japanese market. Much better is the trailer for *Crazy Heart*, starring Jeff Bridges as a washed-out country singer. I look forward to that one arriving in Tokyo. Before going to see it I will get in the mood with a marathon Willie Nelson listening session.

The trailers over, the audience of Japanese women and me settle back for *Up in the Air*.

The opening credits are inspired, a terrific soulful version of Woody Guthrie's anthem 'This Land Is Your Land' playing over retro split-screen views of America from up in the clouds, the natural habitat of Clooney's character, Ryan Bingham. Clooney is in fine form throughout this wonderful film. He infuses his character with a charm and charisma that mask the callousness of the character's personality.

The storyline is one that many people will, unfortunately, be familiar with in their own lives: downsizing, restructuring, and all the other corporate platitudes for firing people.

Director Jason Reitman, who co-wrote the screenplay with Sheldon Turner, does a great job in showing both sides of the story, with the victims of redundancy being given plenty of screen time rather than just focusing on Clooney and the co-stars. We see the range of emotions that the fired employees go through: bewilderment, numbed shock, stoic indifference, rage and despair.

Vera Farmiga and Anna Kendrick are both excellent as the other main characters in the film. Farmiga is Clooney's match, a constant traveller with a bulging wallet full of loyalty cards just like Clooney. But, unlike Clooney and as Clooney finds out too late, she has a 'real' life to go back to when she is off the road.

Kendrick also challenges Clooney. Initially, she seems to be as icily callous as Clooney's character. But a spell out on the road dealing with the real people who suffer the consequences of her work soon humanizes her. The generation-gap chemistry between her and Clooney works very well.

Up in the Air turns out to be one of the most enjoyable films I have seen in a long while. The dialogue is sharp and funny, the cast is great, and the story is well told. Despite the film's subject matter of corporate downsizing, it still manages to be a feelgood movie.

After the film, I walk back home along the road next to the Yurakucho train tracks. The salaryman-filled restaurants are busy tonight, the atmosphere still steamy after the day's rain.

Crazy Heart

Toho Cinema Chanter

La Boheme is a good Italian restaurant set on one side of the central square in the Azabu Juban district of Tokyo. Their snow crab and avocado salad is delicious, as is the Boheme Mix pizza.

A few metres further along from La Boheme stands Peacock supermarket.

What makes the Peacock Store in Azabu Juban different from any other supermarket I have been to is the background music they play. It's not crappy J-pop, or bland elevator musak, or – worse still – a radio station with imbecile DJs and moronic adverts. No, what Peacock usually plays is grand, sweeping, melodramatic music that seems entirely at odds with the mundane act of shopping there.

The music often sounds like the soundtrack to the weepy finale of a romantic film. I keep expecting to see shoppers put down their shopping baskets and reach for a tissue to dab away their tears.

Music of a different genre provides not only the soundtrack but also the essence of today's film, the wonderful *Crazy Heart*. Country music fans will love the music and the feel of this film. When I mention to someone that I am going to see *Crazy Heart*, I don't allow myself to be put off by her withering comment that the film will just be a maudlin tale of "someone whose dog dies, so he starts drinking and then he disappears into the night on the midnight train".

I would still have gone to see the film even if that *had* been the plot.

Jeff Bridges thoroughly deserves the Oscar he won for his performance as Bad Blake, the down-on-his-luck country singer whose career has slid to the point where he is reduced to playing bowling alleys instead of real music venues.

His fan base is loyal but tiny.

His life is going nowhere, his existence shabby.

But he keeps on going, driving alone hundreds of miles across the country to get from one dispiriting gig to another. Injections of brute energy arrive in the form of very funny, expletive-laden phone conversations between Bad Blake and his agent, whom Blake blames for the stagnation in his career.

Although Bridges' acting is top notch, the same cannot be said of his singing ability. He is not a bad singer and presumably he had some coaching for the singing that he does in this role. But the quality difference between Bridges' singing and a real country singer becomes starkly apparent early on in the film when we hear a few moments of the superb Waylon Jennings singing 'Are You Sure Hank Done It This Way'.

If one change could have been made to *Crazy Heart* to improve it, it would have been to include more songs from great country singers such as Waylon, Willie Nelson, Merle Haggard and so on rather than relying almost solely on Bridges to carry the singing duties.

Some reviews of *Crazy Heart* have criticized the relationship between grizzled country veteran Bad Blake and journalist Jean Craddock (Maggie Gyllenhaal) as unrealistic, given their age difference and the gulf between them in terms of their respective lifestyles. How, suggest the sceptics, could such a beautiful, younger woman possibly be attracted to the alcoholic country veteran?

But their relationship rang true to me. Bad Blake may be washed up, but he still possesses the charisma and spirit that propelled him to a career in the first place.

In its ending, the film avoids the usual Hollywood sentimentality. Loose ends are not tied up.

The big plus point about Toho Cinema Chanter is its location close to the soulful salarymanland Yurakucho train tracks, where I head to after the film finishes.

It is still pretty unusual for foreigners to work as salarymen for the big, long established Japanese corporations. The language barrier is extremely high. Not only that, but the corporate culture here and the salaryman mentality take some getting used to. One of that rare breed who has penetrated the workaholic world of the traditional Japanese firm is Irishman Niall Murtagh, a one-time globetrotting backpacker who gave up the wandering life, came to Japan, settled down, and carved out a career as a manager at Mitsubishi.

His book The Blue-Eyed Salaryman provides an entertaining account of his unusual career trajectory. It offers a funny and thoughtful insight into the salaryman world.

Murtagh's take on the Japanese corporate treadmill seems to comprise a mix of respect for the hard work and dedication of his Mitsubishi colleagues, combined with a lingering distaste that never quite goes away regarding the pettiness of the bureaucracy and the school-cum-military atmosphere that pervades the corporate work place. He gives a much more balanced, humanized and fair view of the salaryman life than most foreign commentators. That is probably because Murtagh has actually worked in the Japanese corporate system and knows what he is talking about.

Railways

Marunouchi Piccadilly 3

Japan's national football team exited the World Cup yesterday not with a bang but a whimper, losing to Paraguay in a dismal knockout game. The two teams looked like they could have played for days on end without ever scoring.

Bored rigid by this soporific spectacle, I stop watching at half-time and go to bed.

Because pre-tournament expectations for the Japanese team had been so low, there doesn't seem to be much anguish throughout the land now that they have been knocked out. The lively diners in the New Tokyo Beer Hall where I go for today's pre-film meal certainly don't look at all downcast. This German-style restaurant has a stone floor which amplifies the volume of the clientele's chatter, adding to the atmosphere as you chomp sausage and glug down beer.

New Tokyo Beer Hall is just a few minutes walk from Marunouchi Piccadilly 3 cinema, the venue for today's film, a Japanese production titled *Railways*. The film is written and directed by Yoshinori Nishikiori.

Modern-day Japan is big on railways, and is well known as the land of the shinkansen (bullet train). It is less well known that it was a Scot, Thomas Blake Glover, who brought the first steam locomotive to Japan, running it along an eight-mile track in Nagasaki in 1868. In terms of Westerners coming to Japan and settling here, few can have had such an extraordinary life and impact on the country as Thomas Blake Glover. He was dubbed the Scottish Samurai in a biography written about him in 1993 by Alexander McKay. Then over a decade later Alan Spence wrote a wonderful fictionalized version of Glover's life in his novel *The Pure Land.*

What was so special about Glover? After all, almost nobody has heard of him back in his native Scotland. Within Japan there is higher name recognition for him, although few people would be able to specify exactly who he was or what he did. Glover's immense and as yet largely unrecognized claim to fame is that he was instrumental in arming and encouraging the nineteenth-century rebels who overthrew the Shogun and installed the Emperor as ruler of Japan; he was close friends with many of the Meiji Restoration ruling elite, including Ito Hirobumi, the first Prime Minister of Japan; he played an important role in the early days of the company that would develop into Mitsubishi; and he was in on the beginnings of the Kirin company, a contribution that will be gratefully acknowledged by beer lovers.

Glover's tumultuous life is brilliantly evoked in Alan Spence's book The Pure Land. The novel vividly describes the stark contrast between the often grim and grey northeast Scotland of Glover's youth with the utterly different setting of Nagasaki, where Glover spent most of his life in Japan.

When I bought Spence's book a few years ago in Edinburgh, I was almost put off buying it by the melodramatic cack on the back cover blurb proclaiming it to be a heart-breaking love story and so on and so on. At the time I remember thinking that the blurb sounded like it was designed to be read by the bloke with the booming bass voice who seems to do the voiceovers for all the Hollywood movie trailers.

Years later, I found out that author Alan Spence had originally intended it to be a screenplay rather than a novel. It certainly should be made into a film. It has got all the ingredients to succeed: a great story, compelling characters, historical upheavals, a charismatic hero and in 'The Pure Land' a great title. Apparently the reason it was not turned into a film – not yet anyway – is that Tom Cruise's 2003 film *The Last Samurai* was considered to have cornered the market for historical epics set in that period of Japan's history.

But a few years have now passed since *The Last Samurai* was released. I don't see any reason not to go ahead and turn The Pure Land into a film.

As 2011 is the centenary of Glover's death, that would be an obvious year to release it to tie in with any centenary celebrations. Another reason to press ahead right now with a film production is that Glover's profile was raised in Japan in 2010 when he was featured in a cameo role on NHK's historical blockbuster weekly television drama series, which is watched by several million people.

Today's film, *Railways*, has none of the pretensions to epic grandeur that Glover's tumultuous life inspired in The Pure Land. Yet in its own modest, quiet, understated way *Railways* is an affecting portayal of one man's life choices.

Marunouchi Piccadilly 3 is a good cinema to see it in, its large screen doing justice to the film's occasionally beautiful cinematography. I get a seat in row K, about half-way back.

The story in *Railways* is about a character named Hajime Tsutsui, a forty-nine year old manager in a Tokyo office. He decides to make a drastic career change by quitting his office job to return to his hometown of Izumo in the Shimane region of Japan, where he makes a fresh start by becoming a train driver. This life-changing decision occurs partly as a result of Tsutsui's best friend dying in a traffic accident, which brings home to Tsutsui the fleeting nature of life and the need to take control of his destiny while he still can, and partly because of a desire to be nearer to his mother who has been hospitalized by illness.

Tsutsui is played very well by actor Kiichi Nakai, who infuses the role with an impressively subtle charisma.

The film includes several beautifully framed shots of rural trains crossing the Shimane countryside in western Honshu. At one point it looks like there is going to be a 'love is in the air' subplot when Tsutsui's younger colleague gives a lingering glance over at Tsutsui's daughter, but that storyline is not developed at all. I suspect that the film makers may have filmed some kind of romance blossoming between those two characters, but that those scenes failed to make it into the final cut.

One really excellent scene in this warm, feelgood movie is the job interview. Visually, this scene uses the full width of the screen, with great improvisational-sounding jazz playing as the interview unfolds, the playfully teasing music reflecting the jittery dynamic of the interview situation.

After the film I drift into the nearby Imperial Hotel Bar, a refined and sumptuous setting for a post-film drink. A piano player tinkles away amid the accessible opulence of one of Tokyo's grandest old hotels. It's a good way to end the day.

Brothers

Ikebukuro Cinema Rosa

In Tokyo, probably more than in any other city in the world, you are spoilt for choice when it comes to eating out. It has been claimed that there are 160,000 restaurants in Tokyo. Although that figure seems to have been plucked out of thin air, the city is indeed crammed with an immense number of great eating places, both Japanese and foreign.

The vicinity of train or metro stations is always a promising area to hunt for interesting places to eat and drink.

Roppongi Itchome is one such metro station. Although it is located a short distance away from the main action in Roppongi, it still has a vast range of restaurants to sustain the hungry traveller.

One of the restaurants I frequent in this area is Wayang Bali, a terrific Indonesian izakaya located near Roppongi Itchome underground station. A central row of booths is flanked by more open tables on either side of the restaurant. The lighting is fairly low, without making the place too dark. The music is usually at just the right volume; loud enough to listen to and enjoy, but not so loud that you have to raise your voice to compete with it. It's a good place to go to enjoy an izakaya setting with an Indonesian menu rather than the standard Japanese izakaya fare, wonderful though that is.

The flavours at Wayang Bali are intense and distinctive. The imported Indonesian beer brand Batavia is a perfect accompaniment to the food. Everything I have tasted here is good: Lumpia Goreng, Gado-Gado, Sate Campur, Sambal Goreng Daging, Nasi Goreng, Soto Ayam. I am reading these words off the receipt for the most recent meal I had there. Not understanding a word of Indonesian, I don't know which word represents which food, but it was all delicious.

Just a few yards away from Wayang Bali is another excellent eating place, Inokoya. Inokoya is a Hokkaido-themed restaurant. It is smart and stylish, rather than down-homey, and it has a curiously split personality. On the one hand, it seems to cater to a Western audience through the use of wine glasses for the saké rather than traditional Japanese drinking vessels, the playing of American jazz and pop standards as background music, and a French influence in the dainty appetizers that kick off a meal there. But on the other hand, the menu is available only in Japanese. This does not prevent around a third of the diners being Westerners the night that I was there.

At the next table to ours in Inokoya it was like a scene out of recent movie *My Darling is a Foreigner*, as a keen American in his early twenties eagerly chatted up his Japanese date. To have to listen to the guy's charm offensive was kind of sweet, charming and irritating all at the same time.

The shabu shabu at Inokoya was wonderful, as good as any I have had in Japan. The saké was also exceptionally good. I quaffed a couple of brews from the northernmost saké breweries in Hokkaido. Both were excellent. One was classified a nine on the dryness-sweetness scale, which places it towards the dry end of the spectrum, whilst the other was a five. The brewery name is Kunimare. I will definitely drink their superb saké again.

Though not eating at any of its surrounding restaurants today, Roppongi Itchome is my station for catching the metro to Ikebukuro to see today's film, *Brothers*. I take the Namboku Line as far as Iidabashi and change there for the Yurakucho line to Ikebukuro.

The Tokyo metro system is supremely efficient. You never have to wait more than a few minutes for your train. Getting from one side of this gigantic city to the other is a breeze, provided of course that you can avoid the legendary rush hours when the crush of people inside the coaches can lift you off your feet. It would help if the platform signs with each station's name were written in bigger letters that would be easier to spot as your train arrives and you are trying to see if this is your stop. But once you are in the stations themselves, the signage to guide you is usually pretty clear.

Ikebukuro is in Toshima ward, in the northwest of Tokyo. It doesn't have the glamour and glitz of Ginza or Shinjuku, and therefore attracts fewer tourists. But there is no shortage of locals, as you will see if you ever use the train station here. Ikebukuro train station handles over a million passengers every day. This makes it Tokyo's second busiest station after Shinjuku. It also makes it a considerable challenge to find your way out of the station after you have got off your train.

Having been forewarned about the labyrinthine nature of Ikebukuro station, I came with very clear written instructions for escaping from it.

Miraculously, I make it out of the maze of Ikebukuro station without having to leave a paper trail or do any backtracking. I emerge from the West Exit as intended and walk straight ahead past Bic Camera as far as the unmissably large Oioi department store, where I take a right along the street that leads to my destination, Ikebukuro Cinema Rosa.

As its name suggests, the Rosa building is pink. It's looking somewhat faded these days.

Even though this is a Monday afternoon, the area around the cinema is pretty atmospheric, a mix of innocent-looking restaurants and less innocent-looking establishments such as 'Men's Relaxation' venues with pictures just inside the entrance of the girls who work there. There are also hotels where you can 'rest' for periods of two or three hours, depending on how much 'rest' you are in the mood for.

In the Cinema Rosa foyer, I grab a handful of intriguing flyers for upcoming releases on the Tokyo cinema scene. A weekend of Khazakstan film subtitled in Japanese, anyone?

With this being a Monday afternoon showing, there is no problem commandeering an ideal seat in the comfortable basement auditorium, one of two seats together by the left hand wall with no seats immediately in front. There is plenty room to stretch my legs and no risk of the view of the screen being blocked by another person.

I have never been a big fan of Tobey Maguire but he is very good in *Brothers* as Captain Sam Cahill, the family-loving soldier who comes back from Afghanistan traumatized by the torture that he endured from his captors there. Maguire powerfully conveys Sam's fragile psychological state. As Sam Cahill falls apart, his brother Tommy, solidly played by Jake Gyllenhaal, grows in stature albeit from a very low starting point.

Tommy, previously shunned by his family for his time spent in prison, starts shouldering the responsibilities that had previously been carried by his more admirable brother Sam before Sam went missing in action in Afghanistan.

Other good performances are given by the two children in the film, as well as by the excellent Sam Shepard, who plays the cantankerous father of Sam and Tommy. The soundtrack finely complements the action with appropriately downbeat but good music from U2, David James, Simon Wilcox and others.

When the film ends, *Brothers* leaves me with a slightly disappointed feeling of anti-climax. It starts well but it doesn't quite deliver. The biggest flaw in this film is the offhand, abrupt ending.

"Hey, what about us, we're still here", I think to myself as the credits roll, the film prematurely taking leave of its audience.

The Hangover

Cine Saison Shibuya

Tempura is a style of Japanese food which should definitely be sampled at a specialized tempura restaurant. You can get tempura at other kinds of restaurants, but at non-specialized places it's often not prepared with the same skill and attention that is lavished upon it at a dedicated tempura restaurant.

At a good tempura restaurant the food is fresh, crisply battered and served to you piping hot the instant it is ready. But at establishments where tempura is just one food type amongst many others on the menu, the risk is that the tempura will be soggy, greasy and lukewarm; so unappetizing, in fact, that it could put you off tempura altogether if you have never experienced it prepared well.

A couple of days ago, on a baking hot August day, I had lunch at a neighbourhood tempura restaurant in Mito, Ibaraki Prefecture. Mito is a small city just over an hour from Tokyo by the fast train from Tokyo's Ueno station. It's good to get out of Tokyo now and again.

Mito is a refreshing place to escape to for a day or two, a laidback town with a nice lake to walk around and a beautiful park that is renowned throughout Japan.

Because the saké had flowed freely the night before and I was consequently feeling slightly bleary, I didn't sample any of the sakés that the tempura restaurant stocked, sticking instead to green tea and water.

The tempura was very good: crispy and light and full of flavour. I had a seat at the counter, which is the best place to be in a tempura restaurant, as you can see the chef at work and he will place your order in front of you on the counter immediately after it has been extracted from the vat of oil, hot and fresh. I had various tempura pieces including shitake mushroom, squid, perilla leaf, and some kind of fish which I don't remember the name of. Though down to earth and unpretentious, it was a classic Japanese meal: subtle, delicate, lovingly prepared and delicious.

A few minutes walk from the tempura restaurant stands a very welcome new addition to Mito's drinking scene, the Shige Whisky Shop. For whisky lovers, this place is a gem. I was delighted to stumble upon it in what is otherwise mainly a residential area; it's a surprising location for such a shop.

Inside, the shelves were stacked with an impressive range of malt whiskies from the great Scottish distilleries. Some of the bottles, such as Auchentoshan, had labels that are specially designed for the Japanese market. These labels have a more striking and artistic design than the more conservative labels used in the domestic Scottish and UK market.

Unlike an off-licence in the United Kingdom, at Shige Whisky Shop there are seats and tables where you can order a glass of some of the whiskies they stock. I took a seat and the friendly, cool-looking young guy running the store asked what kind of whisky I would like.

"Something peaty, something smoky. Lagavulin."

"It is young, five years old. Is that ok?"

"Yes, that's ok."

I have rarely had such a young malt whisky before. But that five year old Lagavulin was very good, dramatic and impactful, although not quite as stunning as its older versions. Unfortunately the shop closed for the day just half an hour after I entered it, so there wasn't a chance to sample any more of the store's tantalizing array of whiskies. As I left, I told the shop manager that I would be back sometime soon to try some of the other whiskies he stocks. But for the time being, I had to return to Tokyo.

A couple of days later, back in Tokyo, I find myself in the dentist's chair.

My dentist had injected the anaesthetic a couple of minutes previously. Normally he is pretty laidback, but today he seems fired up and particularly keen to start drilling away at my long-suffering teeth. He appears almost gleeful at the prospect of commencing drilling. I picture him clapping his hands together and cackling demonically.

Today's targets are two molars, upper left. I'm not sure why, but for some reason the dentist's drill doesn't seem so threatening when it is working on upper teeth rather than on lower teeth. On lower teeth somehow you feel more helpless and vulnerable. But on the upper teeth, it's more a case of, "Come on you bastard, do your worst. See if I care!" Such bravado does of course evaporate at the first twinge of pain.

As the dentist drills and scrapes, I ponder what kind of person is attracted to such a career. My dentist is great, I like him a lot. He seems grounded, well balanced, and radiates reassurance. I'm very glad I found him when I needed dental treatment here in Tokyo. But sticking needles into people's gums? Who would want to do that on a daily basis? Peering into other people's gaping mouths and inserting screeching drills into their decayed teeth? What an odd way to earn a living. It's a good thing for the rest of us that some people want to do it.

Having come direct to Cine Saison in Shibuya from my hour-long dental appointment, I laugh grimly to myself when one of the main characters in today's film, *The Hangover*, turns out to be a dentist.

Cine Saison is tucked away on the sixth-floor of a shopping mall just a couple of minutes away from Shibuto Cine Tower, where I saw *The Hurt Locker* a few weeks ago. On my way to the cinema this afternoon I pass three mini skirted teenage girls who are belting out some J-pop garbage on a tiny stage at the street corner of Shibuya 109. A much older DJ stands behind them at the rear of the stage, trying to look interested even though his body language says, "What the hell am I doing here?"

For a pre-film snack I drop into the wonderfully named Freshness Burger, a Japanese fast food chain. Now and then, you come across a strange but good Japanese brand name in English, such as Freshness Burger. But more commonly those Japanese brands with English names tend to be less appealing, like the bottled soft drinks brands Calpis and Pocari Sweat.

From Freshness Burger, I nip over the road to Cine Saison. There is just one screen at this cinema. Turquoise panels curve up the walls to the ceiling.

I sit down in seat J4, towards the back of the auditorium on the left hand side, a good view of the screen from here. Some of the trailers look tempting – *Frozen*, *Zombieland*, *The Men Who Stare At Goats*. Nothing particularly profound, but they look fun.

The same could be said for today's film, *The Hangover*, a crude, boisterous and very funny comedy about four guys who go to Las Vegas to celebrate the last night of freedom of the one in the group who is getting married the next day. The four are a good mix of personalities and the chemistry between them helps the film bubble along nicely.

The film doesn't rely only on non-stop idiotic escapades. It is well paced, with some quieter moments punctuating the hangover-induced chaos.

Ed Helms as Stu Price, the dentist, gets some of the best lines. He also carries off 'Stu's Song' beautifully, a soulful rendering of a crass set of lyrics that makes me laugh even now well after the film has finished.

Bradley Cooper puts in a vigorous performance as Phil, the ringleader of the group, whilst Zach Galifiniakis provides another layer to the story as the outsider who doesn't really fit in to the group, but who nevertheless is an essential member of it. Mike Tyson makes an appearance as himself in which he almost steals the show with his unique blend of sweetness and malevolence. Another high-impact supporting performance is delivered by Ken Jeong as the monstrously camp gangster Mr Chow.

There are a lot of big laughs in this film, right up to and including the wedding scene at the end where the wedding singer scandalizes the assembled guests with his lewd and totally inappropriate vocals and body gestures. The closing credits are good too, particularly the still shot of Stu grinning manically, mouth awash with blood, as he brandishes the tooth which he has just extracted from his own mouth with a pair of pliers.

After the film, I just make it to the bus stop in time for the last number 88 bus of the day. It is scheduled to depart at 9 p.m. and with Japanese punctuality, 9 p.m.

means 9 p.m. So I know that I have to walk quickly from the cinema to Shibuya station if I am to catch it.

Without the crowds, it would be easy. But having to weave through the evening throng slows me down a lot. If I miss the last 88 of the day it isn't the end of the world, but I will then have to catch a bus that will deposit me in the heart of Roppongi, from where I will have to run the gauntlet of touts trying to lure any passing males into the area's seedy strip clubs and hostess bars.

Thankfully, I get to the bus stop just in time, a couple of minutes before the bus leaves.

Safely ensconced in my apartment back in Azabudai, I enjoy sampling a tantalizing trio of recently acquired saké bottles: Maborosi, a fruity saké from Nakao Brewing Co. Ltd. that tastes of apples and which has a steady, smooth, lingering finish; the subtle, fresh and breezy Kamotsuru with its mineral, grapefruit taste; and Ichidai-misen Arabashiri, a densely textured saké from Hatsukaichi, Hiroshima.

So many more great sakés out there, so little time to try them all.

Kill the Referee

Uplink X

Dazed by the heat of the late August sun, I flop into Yamanate Museum of Art. Unsightly blotches of sweat cover large chunks of my damp shirt.

The intense humidity of the summer months in Tokyo has been making coins stick to my fingers when I'm trying to pay for things in the local shops.

I leave my bag in a locker at Yamanate Museum. With that weight off my shoulders, I head downstairs in the air-conditioned coolness to check out the 'Considering Edo Painting' exhibition.

Yamanate Museum specializes in *Kindai Nihonga*, that is, modern Japanese paintings after the Meiji era. However, the current exhibition has a different slant and focuses on paintings from the older Edo period.

Two of the paintings in the exhibition have been designated as 'Important Cultural Properties', whilst three more have been designated as 'Important Art Objects'. It makes me wonder who makes such decisions regarding what is or is not an 'Important Cultural Property'. There are several wonderful paintings in this superb exhibition; it seems pretty random to pick out just a handful for official designation as 'important'.

The interior of the gallery is austere and verges on gloomy, but the exhibition itself is dazzling.

Iwasa Matabei's painting, 'Court Ladies Enjoying Wayside Chrysanthemums' has been newly designated as an 'Important Cultural Property' and features prominently on the promotional material for the exhibition. It's a striking, angular piece with a 'superflat' feel to it that can be found in much present-day manga and anime. The dynamic in this painting comes from the way in which the court ladies and the chrysanthemums seem to be staring each other out. The painting could equally be titled, 'Wayside Chrysanthemums Enjoying Court Ladies', the flowers an audience watching the court ladies on their stage.

But although Matabei's technique is clearly exceptional, it is paintings by other artists in this exhibition that are more emotionally engaging for me.

Among the highlights are Sakai Hoitsu's 'Egrets in Snow' and 'The Moon and Plum Tree'; Tani Buncho's 'Poet's House with Magnolia Kobus'; Yamamoto Baiitsu's 'Shangri-La'; and Hine Taizan's 'Autumn Landscape'.

In addition to these Edo period paintings, there is a small number of more modern Japanese paintings. From the Meiji period the most stunning exhibit is Shibata Zeshin's 'Bokurin Hikka', a beautiful lacquer painting album which you need to lean over and look directly down upon to enjoy the full golden effect of the frames.

From the Showa period, Maeda Seison's 'A Wagtail' stands out, the wagtail in question visually pinned like a butterfly in the centre of the frame against a swirling blue abstract background.

Only as I am making my way out of the museum do I notice that there is a rule forbidding visitors to take notes while they are in the exhibition area. I don't know if that is a mistranslation into English of what the original Japanese regulation states, but I feel a brief pang of guilt because I had been scribbling a few notes as I wandered round the exhibition, blissfully unaware that I was committing a heinous contravention of museum policy.

Nobody seemed to mind when I was scribbling my notes, and none of the museum attendants chase after me along the street when I leave the exhibition and head off to Uplink X cinema in Shibuya.

Uplink X is a must-visit venue for any cinephile in Tokyo.

It's a terrific little cinema seating a maximum of forty people, although there are only six of us in the audience for this Friday's 1 p.m. showing of the football documentary *Kill the Referee*.

I turn up here half an hour before the film is due to start. After handing over my ticket money at the box office, I am given a card with the number 4 on it. This is not a seat number, no no no; that would be far too straightforward. The number indicates that I am the fourth person to have paid to watch this showing of the film. I am told to come back at ten to one, when people will be called in to the auditorium in the sequence in which they bought their tickets.

With twenty minutes to kill, I head over the road to the Lawson convenience store and buy a sandwich to keep my stomach from rumbling during the film. Convenience stores such as Lawson, am/pm, FamilyMart and 7-Eleven can be found in incredible numbers throughout Japan. Known as *konbini*, many of them are open 24/7. They are brightly lit, well stocked and usually have crap but cheerful music playing in the background.

Having wolfed down the sandwich, I return to Uplink X. It doesn't take long for the six of us in the audience to troop in to the tiny screening room. Forty chairs of different designs are scattered around the room, including two or three recliners that are quickly grabbed by other punters who get in before me.

This quirky little cinema describes itself as a 'micro electronic theater' showing digital video programmes. It is part of the Uplink company, which started life as the Japanese distributor of Derek Jarman's films. Uplink's indie arthouse ethos now encompasses not only the cinema but also a café and restaurant, a gallery, and a live music venue.

I have been here at Uplink X once before. It was a couple of years ago, to see *Les Paul Chasing Sound!*, a wonderful film graced with glowing, soft-focus shots lingering on beautiful guitars and on the recording equipment that was invented by the irrepressibly creative Les Paul.

Keith Richards, Jeff Beck, Chet Atkins and B.B. King are among the many acclaimed guitarists who make appearances to share their thoughts and memories of Les Paul, who we see in the film at age ninety playing at a jazz club in New York.

The film traces Les Paul's career from his early country/hillbilly days, his move into the Chicago jazz scene – which is illustrated with some captivating footage of the superb Art Tatum on piano – and then onto his partnership with Mary Ford. There is a brief scene showing the legendary Django Rheinhardt. The advent of radio is vividly described as an exciting new medium at the time. This amazing career and story is anchored in the present through the scenes of the ninety year old Les Paul chatting in the back of the car taking him to his New York gig.

When I saw the Les Paul film, it was an evening showing. In Japan, whenever you get more than around ten people in a room, there will likely be at least one person asleep. In the audience that night, out of a grand total of eleven people, two were asleep even before the trailers started. But today at Uplink X for *Kill the Referee* it's an early afternoon showing and everyone in the audience is fully awake as the lights go down and the trailers start.

It would have been hard for even the most exhausted salaryman to sleep through the trailer for the forthcoming *Samurai Avenger: The Blind Wolf*, with its hilariously over-the-top violence, screams and roars. That film looks a promising candidate for a 'so bad it's good' award.

With *Samurai Avenger* and the other trailers over, *Kill the Referee* starts. Set during the UEFA Euro 2008 football championship in Austria and Switzerland, this gripping documentary humanizes the referees by showing the intense pressure that they work under, as well as the camaraderie that is engendered amongst the referee and his two assistants as they face down the hysterical vitriol of players, coaches and fans.

The film is brilliantly directed by Yves Hinant and Eric Cardot, who do a great job in eliciting convincingly natural, unselfconscious behaviour from the referees who are featured. There's not much playing to the camera by the referees. Instead, we see them dealing as best they can with the technology-enabled scrutiny of a global television audience of millions.

The referees emerge as strong, highly individualistic and charismatic figures, in stark contrast to the UEFA bureaucrats who hold the fate of the referees in their hands through their power to select which referees are going to officiate at the big games towards the end of the tournament.

At one point we see English referee Howard Webb and his assistants having to swallow their tongues as a UEFA representative lectures them in a post-match debrief about a mistake they made during one game, in which an offside decision that was extremely close to call was given the wrong way. But it's only after viewing the replays numerous times from various angles that it becomes possible to judge whether or not the right decision had been made.

The referees must get so pissed off at having to take that kind of criticism from backstage officials who can view every incident from any angle as many times as they want, compared to the referees themselves who have to make a snap decision in the thick of the action.

The nerve-racking drama in this documentary comes across most vividly in the footage of the referees in action during matches, communicating with their assistants via microphones and earpieces. Amidst the pandemonium of a high-stakes game, the referee and his assistants can barely hear each other over the noise of the crowd and the belligerent yapping of the players.

There is a funny moment early on in the film where a UEFA official on the touchline thought for some reason that it was appropriate to tell the referee that it was going to start raining soon. The referee, completely immersed in a frenzied game, can hardly believe that this touchline guy is distracting him with such a frivolous piece of information.

Throughout the film, directors Hinant and Cardot cut very effectively between the different worlds that the characters inhabit, whether it is Michel Platini affably holding court in a luxury hotel in Switzerland, or Howard Webb and his family chatting out on the street in his home town of Rotherham.

The film is very well paced and the music in the soundtrack is used sparingly but effectively. The passion and the atmosphere of the games are captured and shine through. *Kill the Referee* is a great film.

It would have been interesting to see a similar documentary following the referees during the FIFA 2010 World Cup in South Africa that took place earlier this summer. The antics of many of the players in South Africa were worse than ever and must have been a nightmare for the referees to deal with. As the tournament unfolded, it became nauseating to watch hideously overpaid prima donnas writhing on the ground feigning injury only to jump up moments later miraculously recovered.

As *Kill the Referee* is a documentary, it probably won't get much of a cinema release. But when it appears on television it could make referee Howard Webb something of a cult hero.

Exiting Uplink X after the showing, I wander back down towards the heart of Shibuya.

Like so many other areas of Tokyo, Shibuya is chock-full of good places to eat. One of the best is Tharros, a great restaurant located in the confusing web of streets southwest of Shibuya train station. If you can find it – and at least one lost person phoned up the restaurant for directions the one time that I was there – the effort is well worthwhile. It serves wonderful Sardinian cooking, with a wide range of wines from Sardinia and other parts of Italy. The atmosphere is warm and lively.

Even on the Monday night that I was there, the place was buzzing with happily chatting diners. It felt more like a Friday night than a Monday, such was the boisterous carefree mood of the customers.

The background music in the restaurant was Cuban, starting off with mellow son and bolero early in the night and then becoming livelier and more contemporary as the night wore on. But with the steadily increasing volume of lively conversation, the music was barely audible by mid-evening. A slight cranking up of the volume would have been good. The service was impersonal and could have been a tad more enthusiastic, but the food and drink is the main thing and no complaints there, it was superb.

Unfortunately tonight's post-film budget won't stretch to another visit to Tharros, so I head home, with a quick plunge into the Azabu Juban Matsuri 2010 on the way. But the crowds at this festival are so tightly packed that it feels oppressively claustrophobic; I weave my way through the teeming masses as fast as possible to get home.

Back at the flat in Azabudai, I finish off Peter Carey's book Wrong About Japan. Given its limited scope, the book might be better titled Wrong About Tokyo's Manga Scene. Carey is a good writer. At various points in this short book he attempts to share his insights into Japanese culture with the Japanese people he meets, who tend to rebuff his interpretations of their culture; Carey finds this infuriating. Maybe the book's title is right after all.

Seaside Motel

Omori Kineka

I sit down for lunch at the Mita branch of the Uogashi Nihon-Ichi sushi restaurant chain. The food is good here and the prices are very reasonable. The lunchtime menu offers a 1,280-yen sushi assortment that includes scallop, tuna, squid, eel, egg roll and more, with a small soup and a green tea to accompany it.

Well fed, I venture out into the early September afternoon. The long summer heatwave is still going strong. But it's just a short walk, mostly in the relatively cool shade, to nearby Tamachi station where I catch the JR Keihin Tohoku line train to Omori.

The venue for today's film is the Omori Kineka cinema. Omori itself is one stop south of Shinagawa on the Keihin Tohoku line. At Omori, I manage to find the cinema is easily; it's located on the fifth floor of the Seiyu department store just two minutes walk from the station's east exit.

I am here to see the Japanese film *Seaside Motel.* At this Thursday 5 p.m. showing there is a grand total of four people in the audience, including me. The film was released back in June, so presumably most people who want to see it have already done so. I wasn't able to see it back in June. It's good to get the chance to enjoy it on the big screen before it goes to dvd.

Seaside Motel gets off to a dazzling start. The first twenty minutes are brilliant: full of energy, humour, and witty cinematography that introduces each character with an initial close-up of that character's closed eyes, which open followed by the camera jumping back to frame the character's whole body, and then the action in the scene unfurls.

This visually imaginative introduction of the characters reflects the quirky nature of the film, which somehow manages to successfully blend an anarchic comic-book vibe with a more conservative, theatrical approach in which each scene takes place on a clearly defined stage. The stages in *Seaside Motel* are the hotel rooms in which the action takes place.

There is no way that the sizzling tempo of the opening few minutes of the film could be sustained, and the rest of the film ambles along at a more leisurely but still highly engaging pace.

Although there are clear comic-book elements that derive from the film's origin as a manga, written by Okada Yukio, the cast put in terrific performances that prevent any risk of the film degenerating into cartoon superficiality. The relationship between call girl Candy (Aso Kumiko) and struggling salesman Masayuki (Ikuta Toma) is funny, subtle and moving, radiating understated charm.

Each room in the motel, a dingy place in the middle of nowhere, has a different story going on. Director Moriya Kentaro skilfully juggles each story, in the process establishing the motel itself as a supporting character in a similar way as the Coen brothers did for the hotel setting in *Barton Fink*.

If the producers of *Seaside Motel* want the film to become a hit internationally, they should try and get a testimonial from Quentin Tarantino. Tarantino would probably like the film with its off-the-wall characters, garish visual flair and occasional gruesome violence. If he gave his blessing to the film, that could be enough to get legions of Tarantino fans to give *Seaside Motel* a look.

In many Japanese films, the actors leave a lot to be read between the lines; they don't clearly state their emotions or their thoughts. The audience is expected to interpret what the actor is feeling. You can also see this phenomenon on television soap operas, in which a huge amount of screen time is taken up by the actors staring into space, leaving the audience to fill in the gaps.

However, *Seaside Motel* does not feature this staring-into-space phenomenon at all. The actors in this film do not spend time staring mournfully into the distance. The audience doesn't have to try to read between the lines. The action is up-front, spelt out and immediately graspable. *Seaside Motel* is certainly good enough and accessible enough to foreign audiences to become an international hit.

After the film, I head back to Omori station and catch the train to Shimbashi. In this evening rush hour, it's good to be going from the suburbs towards the city centre rather than vice-versa. The trains heading towards the suburbs are packed with commuters returning home after their day's work, whereas my train bound for the city centre is much quieter.

Shimbashi station is not as labyrinthine as Ikebukuro. But it still requires a concentrated effort to find your way out when you are looking for a particular exit.

When I emerge from the bowels of Shimbashi station, I walk through the futuristic cityscape of Shiodome with its glinting skyscrapers and snaking monorail. I make towards the Caretta Shiodome mall. Shopping malls are not my natural habitat, but the ones in Tokyo often contain surprising gems that make it worthwhile to venture inside. Here at Caretta Shiodome, the lure for me is the Shochu Authority shop, an irresistible treasure trove of shochu that also boasts a smattering of tempting saké, wine and beer.

Although popular within Japan, shochu is relatively unknown outside the country. This is a shame, as shochu is a wonderful drink. A distilled beverage made from one of a wide possible range of base ingredients such as sweet potato, barley, rice, buckwheat, brown sugar, or chestnuts, shochu is often compared to vodka. It shares vodka's smoothness and easy drinkability.

But shochu possesses much more kick and flavour than vodka. You can drink shochu with a mixer and many people do, but you get the most out of it if you take it straight or on the rocks.

At the Shochu Authority shop I wander round the aisles for a while before buying anything, just admiring the amazing artwork that adorns the labels of Japanese drinks like shochu and saké.

Eventually I pick out a couple of bottles of shochu.

One is called Sannen Koshu, from Hyogo Prefecture. This one has a chestnut and rice base and tastes wonderful. It is big, smooth and powerful, giving a warm glow like a good malt whisky. The other is completely different, a shochu called Tantakatan from up in Hokkaido. Hokkaido is an unusually northern origin for shochu. Most shochu comes from the warmer south of Japan. The name Tantakatan is intentionally humorous. It sounds like a verbal drum roll when you say the word out loud. The base ingredients are sugar, date and perilla leaf, which gives a light, summery, fun feel compared to the heavier and bolder Sannen Koshu.

Loaded up with the shochu bottles, I leave the Shochu Authority shop. Just along from the shop there is an Okinawan restaurant. Tonight there is a musician standing outside it playing a sanshin, the three-stringed instrument with a snakeskin-covered body whose sound is so evocative of the Okinawan islands.

Further on and nearer the exit of the mall lurks an unexpected find: a Bulgarian restaurant.

Never having had a Bulgarian meal before, I can't resist going in. I walk past a large signed poster of Bulgarian sumo wrestler Kotooshu and over to a table in the corner. It turns out to be a very good meal. The food is similar to Greek cuisine, and washed down with an excellent half-carafe of the house white wine. The restaurant's name is Sofia. It's definitely worth a return visit.

If I do come again to this restaurant, I'll combine the trip with another visit to Shochu Authority to pick up a bottle or two of shochu from that drink's Kyushu heartland.

Micmacs

Ebisu Garden Place Cinema

Ebisu is an upmarket area of southwest central Tokyo, between Shibuya and Meguro on the Yamanote line. If it was just a smart, gleaming shopping and residential quarter then it wouldn't be of much interest. But what gives Ebisu a distinctive edge is its blend of chic materialism, arty sophistication, and its vibrant restaurant scene. No wonder lots of expatriates choose to live in this neighbourhood.

Ebisu train station, like all other sizeable Japanese stations, has got plenty of eating places to choose from. Most of the Ebisu station restaurants are on the sixth floor. You can wander round this compact area and decide which restaurant looks most appealing.

When I ate here once before, the food was pretty mediocre. But someone told me that a thorough renovation had taken place and things were better now. So I decide to pay a visit to one of the recent additions to Ebisu station's collection of sixth-floor restaurants, a Kyoto-style restaurant called O-Hashi, which translates as 'Chopsticks'.

The chef at O-Hashi is brilliant at conjuring mouth-wateringly delicious dishes from the most basic ingredients. Grilled tomatoes in balsamic vinegar and olive oil, for example, doesn't sound very exciting but it is superb. The salad comes with thin slices of pumpkin that are fresh and crunchy, nothing like the soft mush that pumpkin usually appears as. The fish and the lamb are also excellent.

A couple of very decent sakés wash down the feast. One saké is from Nagano, the other from Kyoto. The tea served at the end of the meal is amazingly smoky and pungent, the tea equivalent of an Islay whisky like Lagavulin or Laphroaig.

From Ebisu station a moving walkway called the Sky Walk whisks me efficiently towards Ebisu Garden Place.

I am headed there to visit the Tokyo Metropolitan Museum of Photography (TMMP) for its Onodera Yuki 'Into The Labyrinth of Photography' exhibition. Initially I had been put off visiting this exhibition by the garish, lurid pink, pop junk flyer for it. But the fact that the exhibition is a retrospective of Onodera, comprising sixty works from nine series, is enough to tempt me in and forgive the unappealing flyer.

The exhibition is on the second floor of the TMMP building. It's a large enough space to accommodate the sixty works in an uncluttered yet interestingly juxtaposed way.

The nine series are strikingly different. The photos in the series 'Portrait of Second-hand Clothes' have a rough, earthy texture that makes you want to touch them and hold them; the two-metre high photos of street scenes in 'How to Make a Pearl' make the people in the scenes appear simultaneously carefree, happy and also mysteriously detached from reality; in the 'Eleventh Finger' series, the obscuring of people's faces by lacy perforated paper is a tad gimmicky but occasionally intriguing in its effect; the huge silkscreen prints of 'Annular Eclipse', produced in China by eight craftsmen, are quite stunning; and the unusual perspective of the photos in 'Below Orpheus', with the shots taken from a point near the ceiling looking down to the floor of a hotel room, is impressively disorientating and slightly creepy.

Overall, it's a very good exhibition.

Onodera is certainly no one-trick pony. She has a wide range in technique and imagination, and her good stuff lingers with you long after you leave the exhibition.

Outside, after visiting the Onodera exhibition, it's wonderful to sit for a while in Ebisu Garden Place in the afternoon sunshine under a perfect blue sky. It is fresh and breezy up here, much more relaxing and open than downtown areas of Tokyo like Roppongi or Shibuya. I sit on a bench opposite the squat red-brick building of Sapporo Beer Station and almost doze off in the afternoon sun.

Just a couple of minutes walk from Sapporo Beer Station is Ebisu Garden Place Cinema, which is showing *Micmacs*, a French film by director Jean-Pierre Jeunet of *Delicatessen* and *Amélie* fame.

In the comfortable Screen 1 auditorium, there is a 'No Snacks' rule. I don't know if that ban extends to drinks. The seats don't have cup-holders so maybe they don't want anyone eating or drinking during films. I don't see drinks for sale anywhere in the lobby area.

Just before the film starts, an announcement is made about drinks but my Japanese language proficiency is not advanced enough to tell if we are being told not to drink anything during the showing, or simply that we should place our empty drinks containers in the correct bin at the end of the showing, as is the case in most Tokyo cinemas.

Anyway, I settle back for a drink-less film. If I had blinked during the pre-credits opening frames I would have missed the background scene-setting, which is kind of rushed. What's the hurry, I think to myself, as the film frantically fills us in on the demise of the hero's father and the bullet in the brain that the hero acquires in an accidental shooting.

But once that background detail is filled in, the film settles into a better and more satisfying rhythm.

My expectations for *Micmacs* are fairly low, based on the underwhelming trailer. I thought the film might be too saccharine. But happily *Micmacs* turns out to have a warm charm and a visual splendour that compensate for any potential tweeness. The rich deep colours that infuse the film are beautiful to behold; much of the credit for this must go to the film's Japanese cinematographer, Tetsuo Nagata.

The plot is a simple tale of good versus evil, and won't win any awards for originality. But the appeal of the film is in its gorgeous cinematography and in its cast of offbeat loveable misfits who inhabit a city junkyard and adopt Bazil, the hero, when he loses his job and his apartment. Dany Boon gives a good performance as Bazil. Boon has been compared to Chaplin and Keaton, which is high praise indeed.

There are some good laughs scattered throughout the film. In one scene, the surgeon operating on Bazil asks a colleague to toss a coin in order to decide whether he should try to remove the bullet that is lodged in Bazil's brain. In another scene, romantic music starts to play and then we are given a brief glimpse of the orchestra that is playing it.

I don't think *Micmacs* merits a second viewing but it's better than I thought it was going to be.

By quarter past six in the evening, when I emerge from the cinema, the bright glare of the day has softened to a wonderful blue-grey. The wind has picked up, related to the typhoon that is currently blasting up the far coast of Japan.

I sit for a while on the marble-top border surrounding a group of four olive trees that have been planted in front of Joel Rebuchon's nearby Château restaurant. The gusty wind is whipping through the branches of the olive trees. It feels very Mediterranean, and a lot fresher than it has been during the recent humid heatwave.

I wander over to the Sapporo Beer Station for something to eat. I get a table in the Beer Hall on the first floor. It is mobbed with post-work office parties.

Sapporo Beer Station is a good place, boisterous and atmospheric, with very efficient waiting staff who cope impressively with the large crowd of diners who are there tonight. Once the salarymen are out of their office environment, and eating and drinking freely, the reserved and formal behaviour of the daytime gives way to a raucous beer-fuelled bonhomie.

The meal turns out to be a very satisfying Germanic feast of sausages, salad, potato, lamb, and crab cream croquettes, washed down with a couple of generously sized beers. It's a fine way to end another good day in Tokyo.

Map of the Sounds of Tokyo

Shinjuku Musashinokan

Roppongi Hills is a spectacularly designed world unto itself. It is dominated by the futuristic Mori Tower, one of Tokyo's landmark buildings. Each year Roppongi Hills is visited by more than forty million people. They are drawn here by the shops, restaurants, cinema, museum, and observation deck at the top of the Mori Tower from which you get a breathtaking 360-degree view of all of Tokyo, the immense metropolis extending in every direction as far as the eye can see.

On the fifty-third floor of the Mori Tower, the Mori Art Museum floats above Tokyo like a distant jewel.

An ear-popping ride on a quick and smooth express elevator takes me up there from the third floor. The museum focuses on modern art, fashion, architecture, design, photography and film. The exhibition that I have come to see is titled 'Sensing Nature'. It features large-scale installations and other works by artists/designers Yoshioka Tokujin, Shinoda Taro and Kuribayashi Takashi. The theme of the show is rethinking the Japanese perception of nature.

The flow of the 'Sensing Nature' exhibition is very well thought out, making good use of the museum's space to showcase the different styles of the three artists/designers.

An immediate impact is made by the first exhibit, Tokujin's 'Snow', a large-scale installation in which masses of white feathers replicate a snow drift. The big white rooms used for the first exhibit are wonderfully calm in themselves, regardless of the exhibits they contain. Being here gives me a spaced-out, floating feeling, a sensation that is amplified by the knowledge that I am currently fifty-three floors up, high above the teeming metropolis below.

With this being a Monday morning, there aren't many other visitors. But whilst I am viewing the 'Snow' installation, a lone salaryman appears. He looks like he himself is part of the installation, in his regulation white shirt and black trousers.

Moving on, the long glass table in Tokujin's 'Waterfall' piece is stunning. It is based on the ripple effect of a waterfall flowing into a pool. It has the same hypnotic effect as the natural phenomenon that it is recreating.

Shinoda Taro's section of the exhibition features three new works, the most interesting of which is a new video trilogy of urban landscapes exploring the relationship between human beings, nature and the built environment. This video trilogy is shown on large screens that stretch from the ceiling to the floor.

The foreground water in some of the scenes abruptly meets the floor of the exhibition space; it's as if you could just step forward and be in the water.

Only in one of the three videos does the camera move. That video is filmed in the canals of Tokyo, where the camera prowls below street level like a marine predator.

Tokyo's canals are, unfortunately, nothing like the beautiful waterways of Venice or Amsterdam; they are uninspiring, characterless stretches of water flowing through ugly concrete chutes. It's a real shame, as Tokyo's canals are plentiful and could enhance the beauty of the city if they were valued more.

Shinoda's other two videos are quite different, in that the camera is static but nature moves. The frames are brilliantly composed. Not much happens in these videos. Some of the exhibition visitors just take a quick look and then walk on by with a "nothing to see here" look on their faces.

But if you linger and take in the scenes, their steady minimalism draws you in, even if it's nothing more than green foliage stirring slightly in a breeze; or a car park, empty apart from one vehicle, in which a van drives across from left to right, somehow comical in its understated effect. It's the opposite of Hollywood's exploding car cliché. Here nothing explodes; all that happens is that one van crosses the screen. We do not know where it came from, where it is going or who is in it. But somehow it has an emotional impact. It's a great illustration of the concept that less is more.

Kuribayashi Takashi's works in the third and final section of the exhibition explore the notion of borders between different zones. The most entertaining of all the works in this exhibition is Kuribayashi's forest installation, where you have to bend down and walk under the woodland floor and then poke your head above ground level at certain points to get a bewilderingly novel perspective on the border between the forest and earth below. It's good that the curators placed this installation towards the end of the exhibition, as it leaves you with the feeling that you have actively participated in the exhibition rather than having merely viewed it passively.

Unlike the innovative and interesting works exhibited at the Mori Museum, the cinema within the same Roppongi Hills complex tends to serve up a diet of standard Hollywood and Japanese mainstream fare for the popcorn-munching masses. There are no interesting films showing here, so I venture further afield to Shinjuku Musashinokan cinema, which is showing *Map of the Sounds of Tokyo*.

When I get off the Oedo Line train at Shinjuku metro station, I join a small cluster of disorientated passengers looking at the 'You are here' box on the platform map, all of us trying to work out what direction to take to get out of the station. But the signposting is fairly clear and after a short hike I emerge out of Exit 2 and head towards the Shinjuku backstreets where Musashinokan cinema is located.

The cinema is about thirty seconds walk from the JR Shinjuku Station Central East Exit. The easiest way to find it is to walk towards the big Comme Ça department store and then in the backstreet next to that store, cast your gaze upwards to the second floor on the opposite side of the road where there is an enormous red mechanical crab with moving claws.

I am entranced by this huge mechanical crab. I would happily stare at it in wonder for quite a while. But I get the feeling that the other people in the street would think I was slightly moronic if I did that. So instead of standing there gawping slack-jawed at the crab, a few furtive glances at it have to suffice.

The cinema is on the third floor of a shopping mall. It's opposite a Big Echo karaoke pub, a darts bar and a 100-yen shop.

I buy my ticket and have forty minutes to spare before the film is due to start. Gasping for a beer, I dive into the nearby Dubliners Irish theme pub.

Almost inevitably, a version of 'Danny Boy' is playing when I enter the Dubliners bar. But the music soon gets better and less predictable.

Perched on a stool and clutching a pint of Yebisu beer, I admire a poster reproduction of what is described as the first Guinness advertisement ever issued in a national paper. Some of the claims in the written copy invite a derisive cackle from today's cynical consumer. But the artwork on those old Guinness ads is wonderful and has stood the test of time very well.

Having quaffed the beer, I return to the cinema for a late afternoon showing of *Map of the Sounds of Tokyo*. Before coming to see this film I had read that the plot revolves around a woman who works as an employee at Tsukiji fish market, but who also happens to be a contract killer. She falls in love with the man she has been hired to kill and cannot bring herself to kill him. Not too promising, I thought. But the allure of the movie is that it was shot here in Tokyo; it's always interesting to see how the city you live in is portrayed in film.

The film is showing in Screen 3, an elegant and compact auditorium where there are umbrella slots on the backs of the seats. This is the first cinema I have been to which comes equipped with such a handy design feature. I get here at 4.38 p.m. and am glad that I have shown up on time, as the film starts at exactly its scheduled 4.40 p.m. start time with no trailers preceding it.

The title sequence is similar to Shinoda Taro's video I saw earlier today at the 'Sensing Nature' exhibition in Roppongi Hills, the one with the camera prowling around down at canal level as urban life goes on up above.

Without further ado, the film opens with a restaurant scene where two Japanese businessmen look uncomfortable as they and their foreign colleagues eat pieces of sushi carefully positioned on the naked bodies of tall blond Russian girls who are reclining on the table top.

Isabel Coixet, director of the film, grabs your attention with that opening scene. Unfortunately the rest of the film has less impact, as it slowly but steadily meanders to a trite ending.

Japanese actress Rinko Kikuchi is the star of the film. She is a very good actress, but her role in this film doesn't give her much opportunity to shine. Sergi Lopez, the male lead, looks like he could have done a reasonable job if he had been given a better script to work with.

A good exhibition of stills could be put together from this film, as some shots are beautifully composed and the colours are deep and vibrant. But the film's pacing, plot and dialogue let it down.

Tokyo looks good in some of the scenes and the soundtrack is good, far better in fact than the film itself. As for the dialogue, some of it is in Japanese and some in English. The English language dialogue is not particularly inspired. All in all, *Map of the Sounds of Tokyo* is a case of the whole being less than the sum of its parts.

Maybe I'm imagining it, but the sense of disappointment amongst the audience is almost palpable when the film ends. The film could have been so much better.

After the film, I stay in Shinjuku but cross to the other side of the tracks to where the incredibly imposing Tokyo Metropolitan Government building is located. A smooth fast lift takes me up forty-five floors in less than a minute to the viewing deck. From here there are great views that reveal the enormity of Tokyo. The views out are absolutely stunning.

The best view around here is actually from ground level looking up to the top of the Tokyo Metropolitan Government building. This is Tokyo's Gotham. From ground level, craning my neck to view upwards, the building is like an immense Gothic cathedral soaring into the sky. It was designed by Kenzo Tange, one of Japan's most illustrious architects. Tange also designed other notable buildings in Tokyo such as Sogetsu Kaikan in Akasaka; the Shizuoka Press and Broadcasting Center in Chuo-ku; Saint Mary's Cathedral in Bunkyo-ku; and the bizarre and very distinctive Fuji TV building in Odaiba.

Feeling uplifted and awestruck by the superb Tokyo Metropolitan Government building, I descend into nearby Tochomae metro station and catch the early evening train home.

What Just Happened

Cinema Angelica

At the gym I go to in Ebisu, I usually end my workout with a stint on one of the exercise bikes. Today as I peddle away, I'm trying to ignore the vaguely pornographic sight of one guy in the gym getting intimate with his fitness ball; it isn't clear if he is doing press-ups on it or trying to mate with it.

The exercise bikes are a healthy but tedious way to keep fit. But the time in the saddle passes far quicker when there is a sumo tournament on. At such times, when you are peddling away you can watch NHK's live coverage of the sumo on the small television screen attached to each exercise bike.

But lately even the live sumo has failed to distract me from the dull repetitiveness of the exercise bike. The spark has gone out of sumo with the enforced retirement of yokozuna Asashoryu. Now there is just one yokozuna, Asashoryu's Mongolian compatriot Hakuho, and Hakuho is so superior to the other wrestlers that there is no longer any tension or excitement in the sport; everyone knows that Hakuho is going to win every tournament.

For an introduction to the world of sumo, a good place to start is David Benjamin's book Sumo – A Thinking Fan's Guide To Japan's National Sport. Benjamin's book is a hilarious and brilliant account not only of the surface spectacle but also the murky depths of the sumo world. The first few chapters in particular are laugh-out-loud funny.

Benjamin is probably correct when he says that the best way to start getting into sumo is to watch the NHK live broadcasts on television, rather than allow yourself to be dragged to go see a tournament in the flesh before you have acquired a rudimentary understanding of the sport and some familiarity with the individual wrestlers.

As Benjamin points out, if you attend a sumo tournament without any emotional attachment to individual wrestlers, then the whole event may pass you by in an obese blur. Whereas if you have watched a few tournaments on NHK and absorbed some of the unique characteristics of the sport and its practitioners, then you will appreciate the live experience of a *basho* (sumo tournament) much more.

The author is also right about the addictive nature of sumo and the facilitating role that the NHK live broadcasts play in this spiral of happy addiction. A sumo tournament lasts for fifteen consecutive days. NHK provide uninterrupted coverage of the top division matches from 3 p.m. to the climactic final match at just before 6 p.m.

No mood-breaking adverts are shown. This absence of adverts is a blessing, as it allows the viewer to become totally absorbed in the steady flow of successive bouts. It is very similar in its effect to the days when the BBC held the rights to show England's cricket Test matches, five-day affairs that the armchair viewer could follow day after day in the reassuring knowledge that no matter how tedious the match or how predictable the outcome, it would all be shown, thus allowing the dedicated fan to sink into a contented stupor for the duration.

Anyone who watches the NHK live broadcasts and who has read Benjamin's book will be well equipped to fully savour the fascination of sumo.

After this afternoon's workout at the Ebisu gym I walk along Meiji Dori to Shibuya, stopping en route at Jau Hai Nepalese restaurant for a great meal consisting of sesame naan the size of a baseball bat; big, chunky spring rolls densely packed with delicious vegetables; chicken pancake; sag mutton curry; and a couple of bottles of Nepalese Everest beer.

Happily refuelled, I head on to Shibuya.

In the early evening, Shibuya is buzzing. It is an amazing, vibrant part of Tokyo. You could spend years in Shibuya and never exhaust its endless numbers of bars, restaurants and cinemas.

Without too much difficulty I locate Cinema Angelica, where today's film *What Just Happened* is showing. A verse of French poetry, 'Madrigal triste', is written above the cinema's name sign. There is an undeniable arthouse vibe to this cinema but it is also quite down-to-earth and friendly. The single auditorium has solid, comfy seats.

It's now the third week of September and the heatwave is still going on. Temperatures are well over thirty degrees and the humidity is high, so the cinema's refreshing air conditioning is very welcome.

This is the only cinema in Tokyo that is showing *What Just Happened*. The limited release probably reflects the insider nature of the film. It is very self-referential; a Hollywood movie about the making of a Hollywood movie, but it is brilliantly done.

The film is funny, it looks great, and it is perfectly paced.

What Just Happened has been compared by many to Robert Altman's *The Player*. Both films send up the quirks, nonsense and prima donna behaviour that characterize the Hollywood system. Maybe it's the effect of rose-tinted nostalgia, but the critics' consensus seems to be that *The Player* is superior and in a different league to *What Just Happened*.

Such a judgement seriously underrates *What Just Happened*, which to my mind is equally as good as *The Player*. Both films are brilliant. Barry Levinson directs *What Just Happened* with the same assurance and authority that Altman brought to *The Player*. Robert De Niro's performance as the main character in *What Just Happened* is as compelling and engaging as was Tim

Robbins in *The Player*. Both films are fresh, witty and smart.

In *What Just Happened* Robert De Niro is on top form as the harassed Hollywood producer whose career and family life are in meltdown. Jittery, speeded-up transitions of De Niro driving from one fraught meeting to another reflect the edgy fragility of this period of his life.

In an early scene we see De Niro sitting amongst the audience at a preview screening of *Fiercely*, the fictitious Sean Penn movie that De Niro is trying to produce. De Niro seems genuinely moved and almost in tears as the movie draws to an end, whilst simultaneously he casts careful professional glances around at the other members of the audience to gauge their reaction to the film.

Similarly, in the scene where the director of *Fiercely* shows him the edited version of the ending (minus dog getting killed), De Niro is almost overwhelmed with relief and emotion. He is barely able to speak his gratitude as he shuffles out the door.

It is a masterly performance from De Niro, although he seems to be taken for granted now by a lot of critics. A few years may need to pass before people appreciate just how good he is in *What Just Happened*.

There are a whole lot of other good performances in this film: Bruce Willis as the egomaniac star actor, throwing a violent tantrum and going off to sulk in his trailer; John Turturro as Bruce Willis' weak-willed agent, too terrified of his client to ask him to shave his beard off; Michael Wincott as the director who desperately tries to protect his movie from the brutal cutting that the studio is insisting upon, breaking down in a fit of impotent rage as he realizes that he is not going to get final cut; and Catherine Keener as the cool, authoritative studio executive who firmly commands the director of *Fiercely* to edit out the scene of the dog getting killed. These excellent performances are supported by a great soundtrack that instantly sets the mood for the different scenes.

In his book, With Nails: The film diaries of Richard E. Grant, the English actor Richard E. Grant gives a vivid description of a real-life Hollywood preview screening that was just as disastrous as the one for the fictitious film *Fiercely* in *What Just Happened.* In the chapter titled *LA Stories*, Grant describes driving over to San Fernando Valley for a preview screening of *The Two Jakes*, the sequel to *Chinatown.* When the audience sees Jack Nicholson's name on the screen they go wild with excitement and anticipation.

However, as Grant tells it, the audience soon starts to get restless and fidgety as they realize how inferior this sequel is compared to the original. When the screening ends, the audience members flee for the exits without pausing to fill in the response cards, just like at the end of the screening of *Fiercely* in *What Just Happened.*

Richard E. Grant's wonderfully written book also contains a chapter on the making of Robert Altman's

The Player, which Grant appeared in. The same concerns about whether anyone outside of the industry would 'get' the movies seem to have surrounded both *The Player* and *What Just Happened*.

But even though both films are insider pieces, I don't think you need to be an insider to appreciate them. Anyone with a modicum of interest in cinema should find them easily accessible.

Hollywood may be rightly condemned for spewing out unimaginative, formulaic movies that pander to lowest common denominator audience tastes. But now and again, Hollywood turns out a gem like *What Just Happened* that is as intelligent and sophisticated as any arthouse film.

Feeling hugely entertained after watching *What Just Happened*, I leave Cinema Angelica and plunge back into the hot and steamy September night. I walk along Tamagawa Dori and then turn right along Meiji Dori. The ramen bars and izakayas are still busy with the after-work office crowd.

A Single Man

Wald 9 Cinema Shinjuku

Jun'ichiro Tanizaki would not have liked the shiny, brightly lit gyoza fast food establishment in Azabu Juban that I went to a couple of days ago. The food was pretty good, and cheap, and the service was attentive if very informal by Japanese standards. What Tanizaki, author of a book published in 1933 titled In Praise of Shadows, would have objected to was the unforgiving glare that illuminated every last corner of the restaurant, leaving no room for shadows, mystery or contemplation.

I ordered In Praise of Shadows online. When it was delivered I was mildly disappointed to see how short the book is. At a mere forty-eight pages, it weighs in like an extremely slim volume of poetry. But, like a good volume of poetry, size doesn't matter when the quality of the content is as impressive as it is in Tanizaki's essay on the aesthetics of Japanese design.

Tanizaki's main contention is that traditional Japanese design, based on the subtle interplay of light and shadow, is being threatened by garish Western design characterized by vulgar bright light that eradicates the zones of mystery provided by shadows. The tone of the book is an intriguing blend of chatty observation and more formal criticism.

During the opening few pages I can't help wondering if the book wouldn't be better titled *In Praise of the Japanese Crapper*, such is Tanizaki's preoccupation with the aesthetic superiority of the Japanese toilet over its Western counterpart. But he soon moves onto other facets of Japanese aesthetics and design, such as food, where he applies his considerable writing skills to singing the praises of a dish as humble as a bowl of soup, or the persimmon-leaf sushi made by the people of the mountains of Yoshino in Nara Prefecture.

Tanizaki would probably be horrified by the neon blaze of contemporary Tokyo. Though even in the brashest parts of town, such as Roppongi or Shibuya, there are quiet pools of shadows and winding side streets calmly aloof from the urban bustle.

Here in Shinjuku today on my way to Wald 9 Cinema I am struck by how quickly the frantic activity around Shinjuku station melts away as you walk only a couple of minutes from the station towards the cinema. Wald 9 is clearly visible from the south exit of Shinjuku station, so it is easier to find than Musashinokan Cinema was on my previous visit to Shinjuku.

Wald 9's claim to fame is that it is the first cinema in Japan to install digital cinema facilities in all of its auditoriums. It's certainly an impressive venue. I take the lift up to the ninth floor where the box office is located.

Above the box office counters a curving, illuminated staircase leads up to a balcony stage which presumably is used for celebrity appearances. The staircase is roped off, maybe to discourage more exhibitionist filmgoers from ascending the staircase to address the masses below from up above on the balcony stage.

Opposite that balcony stage, one floor up from the box office area, there is a good café where I enjoy a pre-film draft beer whilst watching trailers for currently showing films on a large wall-mounted screen.

At the box office I buy my ticket for today's film, *A Single Man*. Wald 9 is a good cinema but it has that annoying policy of allocating specific seat numbers when you buy your ticket. Why not just let everyone decide where they want to sit once they have got into the auditorium? The ridiculous thing about the seat number ticketing is that you can end up with some stranger sitting right next to you or directly in front of you or behind you in a largely empty auditorium. But you can't then move to a different seat, because Sod's Law dictates that if you do so, you will move to a seat that some other person has a ticket for and you will then have to move again when that person appears.

A variation on this seating scenario occurs ten minutes into today's showing of *A Single Man*. The auditorium is only about twenty per cent full. There are acres of empty seats available. But because of the seat number ticketing, when a latecomer enters she has to squeeze and stumble past the one other person who is sitting in their particular row. This is not what you want just as the film is getting underway. If the management allowed everyone to sit wherever they liked, there would be much less distraction and irritation for everyone as people would be able to ease unobtrusively into their seat without clambering over folks who are already seated.

Many cinemas allow you to sit wherever you want; if only all cinemas were like that.

Fortunately, I don't have any latecomers clambering over me in my row. The cinema's state-of-the-art digital equipment certainly enhances the viewing experience. The seats are very comfortable too. Jazzy background music plays before the film starts; it sounds crystal clear over the auditorium's excellent sound system.

What a wonderful film *A Single Man* turns out to be.

Colin Firth puts in an Oscar-worthy performance as the main character, a suicidal English professor at an American university. He has decided to blow his brains out following the death in a car accident of Jim, his lover of sixteen years. While hardly a lighthearted romp, the film is not as depressing as its subject matter would suggest. In fact, it is not depressing at all.

A Single Man is very moving. It is also beautiful to look at, with superb use of colour in its cinematography, switching from subdued almost washed-out tones to more vibrant colours according to the mood of the scene.

Violin and cello feature prominently in the soundtrack, perfectly capturing the personality and the state of mind of Colin Firth's character. The soundtrack also makes good use of silence and ambient sounds, as in the scene where Firth's character is sitting in a bank's reception area. He is lost in thought. The small daughter of one of his neighbours comes over and starts talking to him. The kid's mother soon comes over and tells her to stop bothering him. As mother and daughter walk away, there is no heavy-handed symbolic music to tell us how we should be responding to this scene; instead, there is just the sound of the mother and daughter's steps resounding on the bank office floor as they walk away.

The sets look great and provide an atmospheric recreation of early 1960s America. The dialogue sparkles, probably due to its source in Christopher Isherwood's novel on which the film is based. Fashion designer Tom Ford directs *A Single Man* with great sensitivity and focus, maintaining the film's mood right through to the very last frame.

Colin Firth is superb in the leading role, detached yet passionate, viewing his existence with a wry despair that is counterbalanced by a life-affirming dry sense of humour. There are great performances too from Julianne Moore, despite her character's somewhat grating horse-like laughter; Matthew Goode as Jim, whose grounded and sunny outlook on life makes him such a valuable partner for Colin Firth's more broody character; and Nicholas Hoult as Kenny, the student who befriends Firth's character and who attempts to rekindle his appetite for life.

Without any doubt, this is one of the best films I have seen this year.

Screen 9, where *A Single Man* is showing, is on the thirteenth floor of the building. I have to take an escalator back down to the ninth-floor box office area, and from there the lift takes me down to ground level. From the escalator between the ninth and thirteenth floors there are great views of the NTT Shinjuku Building, which looks just like New York City's Empire State Building.

After the film I take the escalator down, admire the view and head back towards Shinjuku station where a few mid-evening buskers are playing to small clusters of onlookers. Most people don't stop to listen to the buskers but a few do; they applaud at the end of songs, whilst the majority of commuters hurry past on their ways to who knows where.

I take the Oedo Line subway train from Shinjuku back to Azabu Juban, the nearest station to my flat in Azabudai. I get back just in time to hear on the NHK news that Japanese novelist Haruki Murakami has missed out on this year's Nobel Prize for Literature, which is awarded instead to Peruvian writer Mario Vargas Llosa. Tough luck on Murakami, but hopefully he will win it next year or soon thereafter.

Norwegian Wood, the cult book that set Murakami on the path to fame and fortune, has been made into a film that is scheduled to open in Tokyo some time in December. Norwegian Wood is a great novel, even better on a second read when its melancholy but quietly passionate atmosphere casts an increasingly powerful spell. The hero, Toru, is a quiet, introverted character who insists at various points throughout the story that he is an absolutely ordinary person, nothing special, when this is clearly nonsense. He is far from ordinary.

The other two main characters are equally compelling: the tragic Naoko and the life-affirming Midori. It's a story of timelessness and drift, a wonderful evocation of the freedom and emptiness of student days in Tokyo. The novel is highly cinematic and should make a great film, so there is a lot of anticipation in advance of director Anh Hung Tran's film version of the novel opening in Tokyo in a couple of months time.

Yunbogi's Diary
Tomorrow's Sun
Sinner in Paradise

Shin-Bungeiza Cinema Ikebukuro

Haruki Murakami may not have received this year's Nobel Prize for Literature, but he will probably win it before too long. It would be a shame, though, if Haruki Murakami becomes to Japanese literature what sushi is to Japanese cuisine – the single dominant icon that obscures all the other good stuff. Also worthy of attention, for example, is another Japanese novelist with the same surname, the unrelated Ryu Murakami. Ryu may be familiar to film buffs for his novel Audition, which was turned into a film directed by Takashi Miike and released in 1999.

Of the two Murakamis, Haruki no doubt has the wider global fame at the moment. Ryu is hardly unknown, though, being a million-selling writer in his native Japan as well as having a publishing deal with Bloomsbury for the English language translations of his books Almost Transparent Blue, 69, Coin Locker

Babies, In The Miso Soup, and Piercing, as well as Audition.

I don't know if Ryu Murakami will ever be in contention for the Nobel Prize for Literature like his namesake Haruki. But Ryu Murakami is a great writer and as times goes by, he may catch up with the more famous Haruki in terms of global awareness amongst literary audiences.

Takashi Miike's film version of Ryu Murakami's novel Audition gained notoriety for the high number of people who walked out of its screenings at the Rotterdam film festival and at other showings. The walk-outs were apparently precipitated by the vivid gore featured in the film. However, in the book there is no gore at all until the climactic scene in which psychopathic character Yamasaki Asami starts dishing out some gruesome amputation. Up to that point, the book only hints at the possibility of darkness and terror without actually showing any; that is what gives the novel its suggestive power.

In fact, the novel would still have been superb even if it did not feature the graphic and disgusting violence of the climactic scene. Ryu Murakami's characterization is subtle, the dialogue is understated, and the plot flows smoothly. The gruesome horror of the denouement is actually superfluous. The novel would have been just as powerful without the Tarantino-esque splatter at the end.

Out of curiosity, after reading the book, I check out the trailer for Takashi Miike's film of the book. The trailer shows someone writhing around in a tied sack on the floor whilst the evil Yamasaki Asami is talking on the phone to the naïve Aoyama. But in the English language version of the book that I read, I don't recall reading such a scene. In that English translation of the book, author Murakami conveys the potential threat of Asami much more subtly.

In the book version that I have got, which may of course have lost something in translation, for that telephone scene Aoyama calls Asami and it is the fact that Asami answers in a deeper and quite different voice to the one which she had used during her audition that should have set alarm bells off in Aoyama's mind. It certainly startles the reader, hinting that there may be some kind of split-personality danger lurking within Asami.

For its shock value and arthouse reknown, Miike's film *Audition* is often compared to fellow Japanese director Nagisa Oshima's *Realm of the Senses*. Oshima is of an earlier generation of film makers compared to Miike. Oshima is revered as one of the leading figures, if not *the* leading figure, in the Japanese 'New Wave' cinema movement of the late 1950s and early 1960s.

It's a Nagisa Oshima triple bill showing at Shin-Bungeiza Cinema that lures me to Ikebukuro in north-west Tokyo today. The triple bill kicks off at noon. So I have to leave my apartment in Azabudai in the morning, with the sound of screeching bulbuls ringing in my ears.

"Keep the moral! Don't throw away a cigarette butt!" shouts a sign posted up by the entrance to an apartment block on the way to Roppongi Itchome metro station.

I arrive at Ikebukuro at 11 a.m. Already there are a few people eating lunch in Ikebukuro Station's noodle restaurants. These early diners probably got up at 6 a.m. or earlier to commute into central Tokyo from the far-flung suburbs; no wonder they are hungry and ready for lunch at such an early hour.

Shin-Bungeiza cinema is tucked away among the garish neon sidestreets next to Ikebukuro Station.

As the living-dead customers trudge into a pachinko parlour near the cinema, the gates of hell open and a thunderous din emanates from the parlour and assaults the street outside. The pachinko parlour doors close after the customers have entered the premises and been swallowed up; once again relative quiet prevails in the street outside.

It's an early October day, quite warm. To the relief of everyone in Tokyo, the year's humidity has mostly disappeared. It is now very pleasant to be out and about after the exhausting extended heatwave of summer.

As I emerge from the east exit of Ikebukuro Station, a couple walk past me going in the opposite direction. The guy has pink hair and the girl is dressed like an anime character. In other cities such a sight might be startling, but here in Tokyo it's par for the course.

Having located the cinema I go in and buy my ticket for the Oshima triple bill. The programme consists of two shorts and one full-length feature. The two shorts are *Yunbogi's Diary* (1965) and *Tomorrow's Sun* (1959), whilst the full-length feature is *Sinner in Paradise* (1968).

Shin-Bungeiza is one of many jewels in the crown of Tokyo's cinema scene. It provides an opportunity to enjoy on the big screen a constant stream of films that includes not only the very best work by specific directors, but also some lesser known works as well.

Whereas Oshima's best known films such as *Realm of the Senses* and *Merry Christmas Mr Lawrence* get widely shown, the films on today's triple bill are less familiar and thus more intriguing.

Tickets at this cinema are dispensed from a vending machine. One of the staff helpfully shows me how to use it when he sees that I am baffled by it. There is a while to go before the showing is due to start so I wander out again into the Ikebukuro backstreets.

Clustered near the cinema are a Nagasaki blowfish restaurant, with several of those deadly creatures swimming around in a tank in the window; an inviting conveyor belt sushi restaurant; a lure and fly fishing tackle shop; and a soapland charging 5000 yen for services unspecified, but which one can easily imagine.

The area is dominated by the amazing needle-like chimney of the prosaically named Toshima Garbage Factory. This incineration plant burns 300 tons of garbage every day. The chimney is the tallest in Japan; its dizzying height ensures that the pollution is carried safely away, high above the citizens down below. For a few minutes I can't help but stare in admiration at this unlikely urban landmark.

Back at the cinema, the decent-sized audience is almost exclusively male. The auditorium decor and atmosphere are somewhat dark and gloomy, though that impression is possibly brought on by the contrast between the bright midday conditions outside and the subdued lighting in the cinema.

I manage to get a perfect seat right in the middle of the back row, which is slightly raised and gives a great view of the screen.

First up on today's Nagisa Oshima triple bill is *Yunbogi's Diary*. The format of this twenty-four minute film is quite un-cinematic. It consists of a series of black and white photographs taken by Oshima during a trip to Korea in 1964. Yet it works very well. The photographs are thoughtfully composed, and startling in their depiction of the abject poverty that was prevalent in Korea at the time. The series of still images are accompanied by voiceover narration by a young boy. Now and then the boy's narration alternates with director Oshima himself, who chimes in by reading some incantatory verse.

This simple structure is strangely compelling. Before the film started, I thought that it might be a bit dull and austere. But the lack of movement on the screen allows the viewer to concentrate on each image and to feel their resonance more deeply than is possible in a 'normal movie', in which directors use on-screen movement to manipulate the flow of our attention.

Also, having two people delivering the voiceover creates a very different feel and dynamic compared to when there is just a single narrator.

The soundtrack is equally inspired. Classical guitar and violin accompanies the more melancholy and reflective scenes, whereas a harsher insistent percussion underscores the more dramatic scenes of turmoil depicted in the stills of troubled 1960s Korea.

The second of today's films, *Tomorrow's Sun*, is a mere seven minutes long. It can be seen in its entirety on YouTube, unless it has been removed by now. After the seriousness of *Yunbogi's Diary*, *Tomorrow's Sun* provides a blast of bright Technicolor and lighthearted fun, but not much else. Apparently Shochiku studio gave Oshima the opportunity to make this short, which is a trailer for a film that does not exist, as a test to see whether Oshima had the skills necessary to be allowed to make a full-length feature.

Tomorrow's Sun is slick and professional, though it looks pretty dated these days. Diehard fans of Oshima will want to see it, but for everyone else this scrap from the great man's table is fairly forgettable.

Much more satisfying is the main feature, Oshima's 1968 film *Sinner in Paradise*. There is a blend of comedy and sharp social commentary in this film. What is being shown today is a scratchy print with static crackle. It's like listening to an old vinyl record. This actually adds to the atmospheric quality of the film rather than detracting from it.

The opening scene is great. Watching this scene unfold, I realize that Oshima truly is a masterful director. To the accompaniment of an irresistibly daft squeaky-voiced song, the three main characters go to the beach, strip down to their underwear and go for a swim. While the three lads are having a swim, a mysterious hand pokes up out of the beach and grabs the clothes that they have just shed, replacing them with another set of clothes that gets the boys mistaken for Koreans rather than the Japanese that they are. This sets up the story that follows as an occasionally surreal satire of racist attitudes. But there is nothing heavy-handed or pontificating about Oshima's approach; he delivers his anti-racist message with frequent doses of humour.

Whoever put together today's Oshima triple bill did a great job, offering us three completely different films, perfectly sequenced. *Yunbogi's Diary* challenges us to focus on and interpret the still images that comprise the film; *Tomorrow's Sun* provides a few minutes of light relief; and then *Sinner In Paradise* entertains, provokes and puzzles.

Watching such a well thought-out triple bill has been a great way to spend this Friday afternoon.

After leaving Shin-Bungeiza cinema, I retrace my steps back to Ikebukuro Station. From here, I catch the Yamanote Line train to Ebisu to pay another visit to the Yamatane Museum of Art. This time the exhibition is titled, 'Nihonga vs Yoga: Betwixt and Between Japanese and Western-Style Painting'. In this context, the term *Yoga* refers to Japanese oil paintings that are heavily influenced by Western paintings.

The exhibition covers the Meiji, Taisho and Showa Periods of recent Japanese history. During these periods, Nihonga and Yoga painters increasingly influenced each other and drew from each other's styles.

Two of the exhibits are designated as 'Important Cultural Properties'. Both are from the Taisho Period: Hayami Gyoshu's wonderful painting 'Dancing in the Flames' (1925) and Kishida Ryusei's 'Road cut through a Hill' (1915). Kishida Ryusei's painting leaves me cold, but I stand mesmerized by 'Dancing in the Flames'; the stylized lava-like flow of the flames casts a hypnotic spell broken only by the arrival of some other visitors who want to look at the picture.

Other memorable exhibits include Umehara Ryuzaburo's 'Autumn in Beijing' (Showa Period, 1942), with its deep vibrant colours showing a Beijing of green nature and blue sky far removed from the polluted metropolis of today; Yokoyama Misao's 'Manhattan' (Showa Period, 1961), its strikingly flat perspective scrunching the skyscrapers up even closer together than they are in reality; two superb winter landscapes which are mounted next to each other in the gallery thereby amplifying their impact on the viewer, Okumura Togyu's 'Snow-covered Mountain' (Showa Period, 1946) and Kayama Matazo's 'Mountains in Winter' (Showa Period, 1966); and the hauntingly beautiful 'Spring Dawn at the Ferry Crossing' by Kawai Gyokudo (Showa Period, 1938).

Still life works of art such as vases of flowers or bowls of fruit have never done anything for me, but somehow Kobayashi Kokei's 'Still Life' (Taisho Period, 1922) stands out. All it shows is one apple in a bowl. Simple stuff. Maybe it is the harmony of the colours, or the way that the bowl seems to float isolated and anchored in the centre of the picture, but for some reason it lingers in the mind.

The highlight of the exhibition for me is one of the older pictures, Saigo Kogetsu's 'Landscape in Taiwan' (Meiji Period, 1912). The foreground trees and scrubland plain give way to a mountain range in the background, whilst a straggling belt of cloud hangs in the air between the foothills and the mountain tops. The whole scene, including the sky, is suffused with a strangely distinctive, understated grey-green tone.

What really differentiates 'Landscape in Taiwan', though, from most other landscapes is that in the middle ground of the picture, between the plain and the mountains, there stands a small factory. But rather than being an eyesore, this factory constitutes a discreet focal point around which the rest of the picture coheres. The factory chimney, for example, mirrors the tall straight tree trunks in the foreground of the picture.

Coming out from the exhibition and emerging back into the afternoon sunlight, I feel light-headed and mildly euphoric after seeing such wonderful art. For people like me who have never studied art, Yamatane Museum of Art provides an inspiring introduction to some wonderful work by a wide range of great artists.

Akasaka, about three miles across town from Ebisu, is my destination for tonight's entertainment. In Akasaka I go to a club to see latin jazz pianist Hector Martignon perform with a group of Japanese musicians. Their set is a brilliant blend of latin jazz and salsa. Back in the day, Hector played with the legendary Ray Barreto's band for six years; he also played with Tito Puente, Celia Cruz and many other leading lights of the latin music scene.

The bar staff at the venue look like they have just returned from a big hair seminar. One of them has a splendid Mohican, a real bog brush, whilst one of his colleagues wanders around turning heads with his enormous mop of candy floss hair in the style of Johnny Pacheco circa 1972.

During the second of the band's two sets, they are joined by a superb trumpet player from Orquesta de la Luz. This guy was sitting just in front of me by the bar for a while before he got up to do his guest spot. His battered trumpet case is adorned with various stickers, including one from Orquesta de la Luz's tour of Puerto Rico. That particular sticker is peeling away; he tries smoothing it down but its sticking-down days are clearly over.

I speak briefly to Hector Martignon at the beginning and the end of the night; not only is he a great musician, he is also a very nice guy.

El Topo

Human Trust Cinema Shibuya

Tower Records in Shibuya is the biggest music store in Japan. There is a good English language book section on the seventh floor, which I will go back to again when I have more time to browse. But my goal today is to get a cd by Oki Dub Ainu Band, before sprinting over to the strangely named Human Trust Cinema to see the even stranger film *El Topo*.

Mission accomplished at Tower Records: in the world music section I find Oki Dub Ainu Band's most recent cd, Sakhalin Rock. The band's leader, Oki, plays a traditional Ainu instrument called the *tonkori*. The tonkori is a stringed instrument without frets. This forces musicians who play the tonkori to rely on rhythmic variations much more than is the case with fretted stringed instruments like the guitar. The sound of the tonkori is quite distinctive, like the harp but tougher sounding.

Oki is reckoned to be the leading tonkori player in the world and the songs on Sakhalin Rock showcase his talent. The title track kicks things off in upbeat fashion. But it's on the slower and mid-tempo songs that the tonkori comes into its own, particularly on the third track, 'Tonkori Monimahpo' and on the last two tracks, 'Flower and Bone' and the wonderful 'Toya', which chugs along irresistibly.

With his Oki Dub Ainu Band, Oki seems to be doing what Afro Celt Sound System and others have been doing in different cultural contexts, taking a traditional folk form and updating it for the twenty-first century. Great stuff.

From Tower Records, I head towards Human Trust Cinema on the other side of the Yamanote Line tracks. Over on that side the streets have smaller funkier shops than the big name brand stores that dominate Shibuya. A taxi rank opposite the cinema building is a magnet for local skateboarders. The area has got a very different feel to the strident commercialism of most of Shibuya.

The cinema is up on the eighth floor of its building. I buy my ticket for *El Topo*, row I, seat 5, toward the back of the square-shaped auditorium. The ceiling is fairly low and the black seats and blue carpet add to the compact feel of the place. A cool, arty crowd is in for tonight's showing of this cult spaghetti western.

In Spanish, 'el topo' means 'the mole'. The end part of the film is about a group of outcast people's attempts to escape from being trapped underground. By a bizarre coincidence, I watch this film on the very same October day on which the Chilean miners begin popping up to the surface after being trapped in their mine in northern Chile for two months. Piling one coincidence upon another, the director of *El Topo* is from Chile. Spooky.

Although *El Topo* was never a mainstream hit, it has had a dedicated cult following since its release in 1971. The film is weird, demented and beautifully shot. There is frequent deranged laughter from the various oddball characters who populate the film. The dialogue is sparse and direct, with only the occasional poetic flourish. The film is all about atmosphere, a vibe which is much closer to the sudden random violence and underlying madness of Cormac MacCarthy's vision of the Old West rather than the relatively sanitized Hollywood western version of that period in history.

El Topo is written and directed by Alejandro Jodorowsky, who also gives himself the leading role. No shrinking violet this guy. In his heroic solitude, the main character in *El Topo* is similar to Clint Eastwood's man with no name in the Sergio Leone trilogy of *A Fistful of Dollars*, *For a Few Dollars More*, and *The Good, The Bad and The Ugly*. But whereas the Clint Eastwood character is introverted and mysterious, the *El Topo* character is an insane exhibitionist.

In some scenes of *El Topo* there is a jarringly effective contrast between the jolly, carefree Mariachi style music of the soundtrack and the grim violence playing out on screen. Lots of bloodshed occurs, although the blood is from the tomato ketchup school of special effects.

The *El Topo* character certainly makes a dramatic exit from the film, which closes on a wonderfully framed shot.

After the film, on the long walk back along Meiji Dori, I pass some salarymen who are lurching along the pavement. A few of them are sprinting to catch the last train home from Shibuya Station. One pair of salarymen sway slowly past me, leaning on each other to hold themselves up after what has probably been several convivial hours of beer or saké drinking. It's one of the great things about Tokyo; you see people the worse for wear after enjoying a night out, but it almost never descends into the violence or threatening atmosphere you get in many cities in other parts of the world.

Koyamaru – L'Hiver et Le Printemps

Eurospace Cinema Shibuya

The leaves on the Tokyo trees are now looking a tired green. It's the second half of October and the heatwave humidity has mostly gone. The bus taking me from Roppongi to Shibuya this midweek evening must be ahead of schedule, as it idles for five minutes at a stop not far from Shibuya even though no one is getting on or off. When it delivers me to my stop by the train station, I get off and find Eurospace cinema down a Shibuya backstreet, where it shares a building with Cinema Vera.

I buy my ticket for *Koyamaru – L'Hiver et Le Printemps* and then head over to Tower Records. A quick rummage through the cd discount bin here on the fifth floor produces one gem in the form of Arizona Motel by the Hacienda Brothers, which is great listening if you are in a *Crazy Heart* kind of mood.

Hacienda Brothers are Dave Gonzalez, Hank Maninger, David Berzansky, Dale Daniel and Chris Gaffney. Chris Gaffney sadly died soon after this album was recorded. The album is dedicated to his memory by the other members of the band. Although a studio recording, it has got a nice live feel to it, whether in the classic country sounds of 'Use to The Pain' and 'When You're Tired of Breaking Other Hearts', or in the more ethereal alt country of 'Ordinary Fool'. As with a lot of country music, the more you drink, the better it sounds.

From Tower Records, I make it back to Eurospace just in time for the start of the film. I had underestimated how much the seething mass of people in early evening Shibuya would slow me down as I made my way from the record store to the cinema.

Screen 2, where the film is showing, has a lecture hall feel to it. The seats don't have much leg room, so for taller people it's a bit like sitting in economy class on a plane. But the atmosphere is helped by some good classical guitar music that is playing in the background.

Today's film, *Koyamaru – L'Hiver et Le Printemps*, is a documentary by French director Jean-Michel Alberola. It's filmed in black and white and is set in the depths of winter in a remote mountain community 200 miles north-west of Tokyo. In Koyamaru the younger generation cannot find work and have to leave the village to survive. This sounds like a recipe for a bleak miserabilist cinematic experience. But I'm glad I have come here tonight to see it, because the film turns out to be wonderful and uplifting.

The different scenes are very well edited. Each scene is self-contained, with the local characters talking about their experience of village life over the years. In less proficient hands, this could have led to a disjointed dissatisfying viewing experience. But the transitions from one scene to another in *Koyamaru – L'Hiver et Le Printemps* are handled very skilfully.

The best example of this is where one of the locals talks about his wartime experiences. When he finishes talking, having reluctantly conjured up the spectre of war and the suffering that goes with it, the next few scenes feature no talking at all, just a series of contemplative shots of snow-filled wintry scenes, such as the roadway cleared of snow along which a shallow stream of water now flows. The camera lingers on this simple but striking image, with the flowing meltwater forming beautiful tiny waves.

At such moments, this film goes beyond documentary and becomes poetry.

It is not just visually that the film touches you. Sound is used with extraordinary sensitivity and detail. The sound of the rain on the car as it drives through the mountains to the village really makes you feel like you are there. Likewise with the crackling sound of the outdoor fire that is lit in ritual celebration; the immediacy of it almost makes you feel warm just hearing that crackling sound.

The director and his minuscule crew succeed in getting some of the locals to open up on camera despite their apparent taciturn natures. One such local in one of the scenes sits outside and plays his bamboo flute, offering interesting reminiscences about the days when flute playing was in fashion in Japan and people would have five or six different flutes to choose from according to the feel of the song that they were playing.

In another scene, an old woman says that she doesn't want to be filmed, to which a local replies that it's too late and she's already being filmed.

On the other hand, a more extroverted Bulgarian man who has moved his family to the area clearly relishes having the camera upon him as he exuberantly declaims his awe at the wonder of nature in Koyamaru.

In the credits for the film, Ayako Oko gets a mention for 'Local assistance'. If she is the person who is the film's interviewer, she deserves huge credit, as the interviewer is the person who so effectively gets the locals to reply in detail rather than monosyllabically to the interview questions. Through gentle encouragement, the interviewer also helps the locals to act naturally when the camera is upon them.

At one point during the film a video clip is shown of the shinkansen from Tokyo that serves the region of rural Japan where Koyamaru is located. On the clip you can hear the on-board announcer saying that the next stop is Echigo Yuzawa. Echigo Yuzawa is a magical place. I travelled there last winter on the shinkansen from Tokyo's Ueno Station. It was one of the most enjoyable and memorable trips I have had in Japan.

That December day at Ueno station while we were waiting for the train that would take us to Echigo

Yuzawa, an old man was standing on the platform practicing his golf swing with an imaginary golf club. This seemed to be considered normal behaviour, given the lack of attention paid to him by other passengers. I was tempted to test the boundaries of perceived 'normal' behaviour by kicking an imaginary football to score a goal and then exclaiming "Get in there!", but I thought better of it. The arrival of the shinkansen train taking me and my companion to the mountains of Echigo Yuzawa meant there wasn't time to do it anyway.

The shinkansen pulling into the station was named *Tōki*, which means crested ibis, a rare species of bird that has been reintroduced to Sado Island by the Crested Ibis Preservation Society.

Ten minutes out of Ueno station a superb view opened up to the southwest of snow-covered Mount Fuji etched against the clear blue winter sky. No matter how familiar an icon Mount Fuji is, it is still a thrilling sight. The shinkansen zipped effortlessly through bucolic green lowlands as far as Takasaki, where it entered a tunnel from which it emerged into a more rugged terrain of forests and boulder-strewn rivers.

Up ahead lay another tunnel, one immortalized by Nobel Prize-winning Japanese novelist Yasunari Kawabata in his novel Snow Country, with his famous opening line about a train coming out of a long tunnel into the Snow Country.

Kawabata's Snow Country is the downbeat but mesmerizing tale of the relationship between

Shimamura, a dilettante from Tokyo, and Komako, a geisha at the hot spring resort which Shimamura visits in the winter and autumn. The emotions in this strange relationship range from passionate commitment to chilly detachment, and are drawn with great subtlety by author Kawabata.

It's a wonderful book. The geographic setting in which the story unfolds is as much a character as Shimamura and Komako, the two main protagonists.

The Snow Country of the title is a mountainous region of Japan that receives immense amounts of snowfall for several months of the year. Snowdrifts pile up several feet high, giving the region a physical isolation that mirrors the emotional isolation of the main characters in the book.

The understated simplicity of the language of Snow Country resembles Hemingway's pared down style, whilst the indifference of the stunningly beautiful landscape has echoes of Albert Camus' early stories set in North Africa, such as Noces à Tipasa and Le vent à Djemila. Kawabata's descriptions of the mountains, snowfall, cedar groves, and the light fading from the day, are written with a poetic power that lingers long after you have put the book down.

Back on the shinkansen, the abrupt transition from the snowless world before the tunnel into the deep snow drifts of Echigo Yuzawa at the other end of the tunnel was stunning and surreal.

We got off the train at Echigo Yuzawa. Outside the station the snow was falling in slow motion, creating a strangely serene and calming effect.

Lunch beckoned, so after a few moments of gazing dreamily at the falling snow we headed back into the station where we enjoyed a delicious meal of pork, rice, and fish soup at Hosaku restaurant. The food was good and the saké was a solid if unspectacular brew called Kanetsugu, named after a local sixteenth-century samurai.

However, the real saké action was just about to begin.

"If this button is pushed, Alcohol will come out."

Those magic words sounded good to me. We were now in the saké tasting area of Ponshukan, an irresistible space in the station basement dedicated to saké and other local food and drink products. There was a vast array of Niigata sakés to sample.

The system for tasting saké here was efficient and ingenious. We paid the modest sum of 500 yen to the person at the desk, who gave us a small tasting cup called an *o-choko* and five counters which we fed into the slot of the container that held the saké that we wanted to sample.

Simply feed in the counter, place the o-choko under the tap, press the button and out flows some of the most wonderful saké you will ever taste. We had found saké heaven.

We sampled five different sakés, all of which were very good. The best were Kirinoto, a smooth and luxurious honjozo from Uonuma; Komokoyuki, a fresh and elegant junmai ginjoshu apparently sold only in Echigo Yuzawa; and the extraordinary Fukugao, matured in whisky barrels which give it a warm and lingering whisky-like glow rarely associated with saké.

It was tempting to stay all day in Ponshukan in the bowels of the train station, glugging saké. But the inn's mini-bus was waiting to take us to our accommodation, Chobokaku Yuimakura. *Chobokaku* means an inn with a view. The name *Yuimakura* is made up of three elements: Yu (hot water – referring to the onsen), Ima (a lounge, since each room is large and comes with a separate lounge and a bedroom so that you feel at home) and Kura (a traditional style storehouse, after which the building that houses the dining area and the gallery upstairs is designed).

Chobokaku Yuimakura has a superb location, perched on a hillside overlooking the valley of Echigo Yuzawa and the majestic mountain ranges that flank the valley. There are only three rooms in the inn, which gives an intimate feel to the place. The rooms have two levels and are built with wooden beams sourced from old houses in the area. There is a private bath in each room so that guests can enjoy soaking and steaming just with their companion, rather than in a public bath with a bunch of strangers.

Pristine glistening snow was piled up several feet deep outside our room. It was good to sit inside and watch the snow falling outside the window.

A bewildering choice of background music was available over the room's music system, including excellent 'modern jazz' that was playing when we were shown to our room. Other background listening choices were more intriguing: 'Insects Singing', 'English Shower', and 'Counting the Sheep'. The latter consisted of a man with a soothing voice saying "484 sheep, 485 sheep, 486 sheep…"

The evening meal was excellent, washed down with a light and subtle Makihata saké.

The next day we got into the bath-breakfast-bath onsen routine. The sun came out and dazzled with fantastic views of white mountains and the town down in the valley below. We could see the train tracks heading off to the tunnel through which you exit the Snow Country and return to the soft balmy climes of Tokyo.

But before returning to the big city, another visit to Ponshukan was called for. When we went to check out of the inn, I couldn't see our boots anywhere. As we wondered where our footwear had disappeared to, one of the staff emerged from a back room and handed us our boots, the insides of which had been warmed for us.

So much snow had fallen during the night that the mini-bus from the day before couldn't make it up the twisting access road to the inn, so a taxi was ordered for us instead. It dropped us off back at Echigo Yuzawa station, where we made a beeline for the Ponshukan saké tasting area.

We handed over 500 yen and sampled another five sakes. Then we lined our stomachs with a decent soba meal at a nearby restaurant before returning to sample another five sakés.

A couple of those local sakés were outstanding: Juku, a splendid brew from Tamagawa that is matured in snow for ten months, and Waraku Goson Chokara, a very dry, but smooth and refreshing, honjozo from Nagaoka.

We had completed our saké odyssey in Snow Country. We'd tasted fifteen brews from all over the Niigata region without even leaving Echigo Yuzawa station. When the time came for our train to depart, it was a wrench to leave the Snow Country and return to Tokyo.

Echigo Yuzawa is a different world; it's hard to believe that it's only just over an hour away from Tokyo.

Kaigenrei

National Film Center

I cut a forlorn figure as I tramp through the streets of Ginza in the pouring rain, killing time before the 7 p.m. showing of director Kiju Yoshida's 1973 film *Kaigenrei* at the National Film Center.

The National Film Center is just a minute's walk from Exit 1 of Kyobashi metro station. Unfortunately, at the cinema ticket counter I am told to come back at 6.30 p.m. to buy a ticket. It's not clear why they can't sell me a ticket at 5 p.m. rather than at 6.30 p.m. It's a tad disappointing, as I had come to the cinema early to make sure I got a ticket in case the showing sold out.

So, ticketless at 5 p.m., I take refuge from the bucketing rain by dropping into an Excelsior café near the cinema. In the café I get one of good seats facing the window. From this cosy sanctuary I watch the rain crashing down on the pavement outside, which is much more enjoyable than being out on the street and soaked by it.

The great Japanese writer Soseki Natsume writes early on in his book The Three Cornered World about how you need to distance yourself from certain experiences, like getting caught in a downpour, in order to appreciate the poetry of such incidents. Sitting in this warm café in Ginza, drinking a cappuccino and wolfing down a scone, I feel I know what Soseki means. Simply being inside looking out, rather than being outside looking in, renders the wet Ginza night poetic rather than just plain miserable.

Back at the National Film Center the ticket costs only 500 yen, about a third of the usual price for a Tokyo cinema. It's an impressively large auditorium. Most of the seats at the back are already taken, so I sit down near the front. This is the first cinema I have been to in Tokyo where there is a uniformed security guard standing next to the screen during the minutes prior to the start of the film. I'm not sure why he is there; the audience members seem an arty bunch, unlikely to erupt into spontaneous disorder.

Kaigenrei is showing as part of a Kiju Yoshida retrospective that has been running throughout October at the National Film Center. Yoshida is an acclaimed figure on the Japanese arthouse film scene, and the grimly austere *Kaigenrei* gives an indication of his genius.

Brilliantly imaginative compositions characterize the film. The action proceeds at a snail's pace, but visually *Kaigenrei* is extraordinarily striking. In early scenes, shots are framed with huge expanses of empty foreground, with the sole character way off in the background. This really draws your eye into the frame. Almost every scene has several different camera points of view, throwing each character into relief as they speak.

Lead actor Rentaro Mikuni gives a charismatic performance as the doomed revolutionary Ikka Kita. His character's troubled psychological state is mirrored by the wonderfully sparse, jangly, discordant soundtrack by avant-garde composer Ichiyanagi Sei.

The feel and outlook of this black and white film is unrelentingly bleak. But as an exercise in style by a master director, it definitely merits the effort of sitting through it.

Having swallowed my dose of serious arthouse culture for the day, I reward myself post-film with three excellent sakés. First up is the impactful Amabuki from Saga Prefecture, with its autumnal flavour of pears and a finish that warms your throat and chest. Next up is the elegant, understated and very good Maboroshi-no-taki from Kurobe, Toyama. I conclude my saké session with Ofuku-masamune from Niigata, which is dry and slightly sharp but still smooth, with a strong afterglow and a long warming finish.

The dismal rain-soaked streets of Ginza from earlier in the day seem long ago and far away.

Ascenseur Pour L'Echafaud

Theatre Image Forum

Theatre Image Forum lurks down a sidestreet off Aoyama Dori, around ten minutes leisurely walk from Shibuya train station. The quirkiness of this cinema's architecture – a stark grey exterior lightened and softened by a plethora of circular and oblong windows – reflects the idiosyncratic programming, which features not only contemporary arthouse fare but also very welcome showings of classics such as tonight's treat, French director Louis Malle's superb 1958 film, *Ascenseur Pour L'Echafaud.* It's such a pleasure to see a masterpiece like this up on a reasonably sized screen in a cinema rather than just watching it at home on dvd.

Malle's film is showing tonight in the smaller of the cinema's two auditoriums, the one on street level with a capacity of sixty-four. There is a bigger auditorium downstairs. The seats here at Theatre Image Forum are more comfortable, and there is more leg room than at Eurospace, one of the other Shibuya arthouse cinemas.

I get a seat on the back row, from where I have an excellent view of latecomers getting entangled in, and struggling to fight their way through, the broad black curtain which is drawn across the auditorium's entrance door once the showing starts.

Before the lights go down for the trailers, someone in the audience who is sitting a few rows in front of me suddenly jerks his head back. It seems to be a deliberate motion.

What the hell is he doing, I wonder. Unfortunately I soon find out.

He is rooting around in his nostrils and pulling out his nasal hair. Each time he uproots a hair, his head jerks back from the force of the chosen hair being uprooted from its nasal lair. It's as if he is suffering whiplash from a car crash impact.

After each uprooting he admires his trophy, rolling each plucked hair for a few seconds between thumb and forefinger before flicking it to the floor and commencing the next rummage up his own nostrils.

I'm glad I'm not sitting next to him.

The sixty-four seater auditorium is adjacent to the ticket counter. I had no idea the auditorium was even there at all as I stood by the ticket counter waiting to get in. When one of the cinema employees opened the door to what turned out to be the auditorium, I assumed he was just opening the door in order to get into a back office.

The auditorium has quite a cosy atmosphere, due at least partly to its unobtrusive, hidden presence. Coming across it, I feel a bit like Harry Potter discovering Platform 9¾ at King's Cross train station in London.

Jeanne Moreau is the charismatic star of *Ascenseur Pour L'Echafaud*. It is a sublime film. One of the great scenes in it has Moreau wandering the streets of Paris looking in vain for her lover, set to a wonderful soundtrack by Miles Davis. In fact, the music is extraordinarily good and gives the film an added depth and dimension that contributes hugely to the film's status as a masterpiece.

Apparently, Miles Davis and band recorded the whole soundtrack during the course of a single night in Paris in 1957, in the company of Jeanne Moreau and director Louis Malle. The other musicians are Barney Wilen on tenor sax, René Urtreger on piano, Pierre Michelot on bass and Kenny Clarke on drums. All the musicians are superb. Pierre Michelot makes an outstanding contribution with his terrific bass lines underpinning several scenes. If ever there was potential to make a movie about the making of a movie, it would be this one: the champagne-fuelled gathering of Miles Davis and his band, Jeanne Moreau and Louis Malle for their all night jazz session in 1950s Paris.

Jeanne Moreau is captivating throughout the film. Other good performances are given by Yori Bertin as the vivacious Véronique, and Maurice Ronet as Julien Tavernier. Director of photography Henri Decae also deserves lavish credit for sustaining the film's entrancing mood of sensual despair.

When the film ends, I walk home from Shibuya in the autumn night. A gusty wind is blowing. Tree branches are swaying. The first few dry leaves of the season drift along the quiet night-time streets. Back at my apartment in Azabudai, I end the day with a warming whisky from Osaka Prefecture's Yamazaki distillery.

All God's Children Can Dance

Cinemart Roppongi

Some people claim that Haruki Murakami's stories are un-filmable. But to me, his stories seem highly cinematic and it is puzzling why so few of his works have been made into films. Just because there have been a couple of disappointing attempts to render Murakami's stories on film doesn't mean that the stories themselves defy the medium of cinema.

Unfortunately, the film *All God's Children Can Dance* provides a lackluster rendering of the Murakami short story on which it is based. I won't choose to watch *All God's Children Can Dance* again. The film does succeed in leaving you with a certain melancholy warmth, just not enough to merit a repeat viewing.

The main weakness of director Robert Logevall's film is the editing. Scenes seem truncated and put together with little regard to pacing or flow. It's the kind of editing you expect to see in music videos or television ads, where everything has to be compressed into a tight time limit. Such an approach fails to do justice to the languor of Murakami's writing.

But on the plus side, some of the compositions in *All God's Children Can Dance* are striking, and the deep rich colours that suffuse many of the scenes are beautiful. The acting is good, by the whole cast. The lead actor, Jason Lew, has been criticized for lacking charisma but I think that accusation misses the point; his character is a layabout slacker who is not meant to radiate charisma. Joan Chen and Tzi Ma are excellent and Sonja Kinski is okay.

The score's low key elegiac music playing across desolate Los Angeles streetscapes perfectly complements the downbeat feel of the film. But the general tedium and inconsistent quality of *All God's Children Can Dance* is rammed home by the narrator's sign-off, which provides a trite ending to this misfiring film.

I watch the film at Cinemart Roppongi, a venue which is tucked away in the backstreets of Roppongi. Screen 2, where the film is showing, is a great little auditorium with very dark grey walls and ceiling, and seats with purple upholstery. There is loads of leg room, which is a boon for taller moviegoers.

After the film I head down the hill from the area containing the fleshpots of Roppongi to the more wholesome surroundings of Azabu Juban. There I enjoy a dinner of tuna skewers, fried chicken, and seafood salad at a very good Okinawan restaurant on the same street as Hasegawa saké shop. I wash down the delicious food with Orion beer, a brand I don't normally bother with as I find it pretty bland. But tonight

I'm in the mood for beer rather than the awamori that I usually go for in this or any other Okinawan restaurant.

Awamori is a wonderful drink. It deserves to be much better known internationally than it is. It is a distilled rice liquor that tends to get categorized as merely a sub-genre of shochu. But this is unfair, because awamori is very different from shochu.

Awamori comes from Okinawa, whereas shochu can come from almost any part of Japan. Also, awamori uses a different type of rice than is used in the shochu production process. The great taste of awamori and the countless variations that are available from the thirty or forty awamori distilleries in Okinawa make awamori a unique and marvellous drink that should be celebrated on its own terms and not treated merely as a shochu variant.

The best awamori I have ever tasted is the 10 Year Old version of Kumesen – a big, bold, wonderful awamori from beautiful Kume Island. That 10 Year Old Kumesen is superb. Like a tremendous Scottish malt whisky, it assails your palate with powerful flavour. It then delivers a warm glow as it goes down.

Visitors to the awamori distillery on Kume Island can sample Kumesen of various ages and buy whichever ones appeal. The one time I visited the distillery, I sampled all that was on offer and became light-headed just on the free samples. The 10 Year Old, though, was definitely worth carrying back to Tokyo to savour it.

That superb awamori provided a fine lingering taste of the Okinawan islands when I got back to the gigantic metropolis of Tokyo.

Season of the Sun

Laputa Asagaya

Benda Bilili

Kichijoji Baus Theater

Roppongi is the last place in Japan I would choose to be at 7.30 a.m. on a fresh and beautiful November morning like this one. Sleazy guys and their dates are lurching along the grubby streets in a post-party, pre-hangover stupor. Fortunately I am just passing through this seediness. I'm on my way to the station to catch the Odeo Line train to Shinjuku. From there, the Chuo-Sobu line train will take me to Asagaya, a more relaxing and charming part of Tokyo than Roppongi.

At Asagaya a beguiling network of traffic-free alleys lined with ramen bars, sushi restaurants and funky cafés awaits me as I emerge from the north exit of the station.

The alleys are silent this early in the morning.

On the south side of the tracks a dozen old men are clustered together around a pond fishing. The only sound is the occasional crow cawing and one passer-by wearing wooden clogs which clack on the street as he walks by. Early morning Asagaya is peaceful and pretty; it seems a world away from Roppongi.

Laputa Cinema is my destination. What a marvellous cinema it turns out to be, a small and cosy 48-seater with comfortable green seats and a beautiful polished wooden floor. The building's architectural style is quirky and distinctive. It is surrounded by trees and bushes that give it a warm natural feel which is rare amongst Tokyo cinemas.

Laputa is a perfect arthouse venue in a lovely setting full of old Tokyo charm.

At Laputa, I start heading up the stairs to the second floor where the cinema is, not realizing that the ticket counter is on the ground floor. The person at the ticket counter must have seen me going up the stairs, as she comes out and calls me back. In a very friendly way she tells me that I need to buy the ticket before going up to the second floor.

Even the ticket for the film is aesthetically pleasing. It features a photo of the stars of today's film, Yoko Minamida and Hiroyuki Nagato. Superb old Japanese music is playing in the background before the film starts.

I am here to see *Season of the Sun*, a 1956 film directed by Takumi Furukawa. It is based on the novel of the same name by Shintaro Ishihara, who from 1999 to the present day has been the outspoken and controversial Governor of Tokyo. Ishihara makes a brief appearance in the 1956 film as a footballer, an appearance so fleeting that I would have missed it had it not been for a woman sitting a couple of rows in front of me in the audience who helpfully exclaims "Shintaro" when he appears on screen.

A classical guitar score adds a lot to the languid yet passionate feel of this terrific film. The cinematography is superb, evidenced right from the opening scene of the film with a close-up of a horn sounding before a widening of the frame to include the boxing gym people down below. Then, in the first indoor scene, the card game between the young boxers is brilliantly filmed. The camera either looks up at each protagonist or views them on the level with slick editing as each player is focused on in turn. The length of the card-game scene is perfectly timed, neither drawn-out nor hurried.

The atmospheric, smoke-filled dancehall scenes with jazz playing for the dancers are also beautifully filmed. It is only in the beach and open sea scenes where the limitation of black and white film is apparent. Those scenes cry out for deep blue colour tones for the sea and the sky.

Although *Season of the Sun* features no explicit sex, it is still powerfully erotic. The film is a great illustration of the power of suggesting something rather than showing it.

The ending of the film shows the male lead stomping off down a road, beyond which we see a sprawling urban scene for the first time. Until this final point of the film, the background scenery comprises only idyllic seaside resorts or the open sea upon which the lovers go sailing. But the abrupt showing of anonymous urban sprawl at the end of the film subtly yet powerfully accentuates the loneliness and alienation of the main character.

After the film at Laputa I retrace my steps back to Asagaya station. From there I take the train to Kichijoji, the third stop from Asagaya in the direction of Mitaka. At Kichijoji I accidentally go first to the wrong cinema, one which is very close to Baus Theater, my intended destination. Baus Theater, which I find without too much further difficulty, is located right at the top of Sun Road shotengai.

Screen 3 at Baus is, like Laputa earlier today, a cosy little auditorium. The Baus auditorium is an oblong shape with an unusual padded corrugated ceiling.

Benda Bilili is the film I have come to see at Baus Theater. Very similar in feel to *Buena Vista Social Club*, the film follows the formation of a band of destitute paraplegic musicians in Kinshasa in the Congo through their rehearsal sessions in the grounds of the Kinshasa zoo and their subsequent success with western audiences.

The Congolese music in this film is superb. Ricky, the band leader and main singer, is an inspirational figure. Roger, one of the musicians, produces an amazing sound from a length of wire attached to an empty tin can.

The Kinshasa street scenes are vividly shot, showing some of the musicians homeless and sleeping on the street. This contrasts jarringly with a later scene in which the musicians on tour meet an Argentine ambassador and his wife at a glittering event that looks like the Ferrero Rocher ambassador's party adverts. Triumphant concert scenes from European world music festivals provide the uplifting climax of this wonderful film. *Benda Bilili* is a magnificent film and deserves to achieve the same success as *Buena Vista Social Club*.

Feeling uplifted after *Benda Bilili* and refreshed from a few hours spent in two of Tokyo's most appealing neighbourhoods, I head to my local yakitori in Azabudai for something to eat. During the week, this yakitori's clientele consists almost exclusively of groups of salarymen. But on weekends, like today, a much more varied crowd comes in. There is always a good atmosphere in this yakitori. Orders get shouted by the waiters back to the kitchen, and the kitchen shout back their acknowledgement of the orders. Tonight's meal comprises chicken and leek skewers, skewered hearts, skewered goya, and baked potato with cheese and bacon. I wash everything down with a couple of Kirin beers.

The last time I was at this yakitori I brought along a German friend who was on his first visit to Japan. He wanted to experience a distinctively Japanese meal so I brought him here. At first he was reluctant to try the skewered hearts, but after trying them he loved them and wolfed down several more skewers as the night wore on.

We drank ima shochu as well as beer that night. After the meal, as we spilled out from the yakitori onto the street, there was a great view of the Tokyo Tower off to the right, spectacularly illuminated purple in the evening darkness.

13 Assassins

Cinemart Roppongi

There are only three people in the audience this Sunday morning for the 11 a.m. showing of Japanese director Takashi Miike's film *13 Assassins*. I'm sitting on one side of the auditorium, whilst two women are sitting together on the other side.

Before the film starts I flick through my copy of Metropolis, the weekly what's on magazine for Tokyo. The quality of writing in Metropolis is very good, particularly by regular writers such as art critic C.B. Liddell, restaurant reviewer Sara Cortina, and Tokyo bar-hopper James Hadfield. The latter seems to have the enviable job of getting paid to drink his way around this superb city and then report on his findings.

The lights go down and *13 Assassins* starts.

Most of this samurai film is great. It is only in the battle scene of the final third of the film that it becomes somewhat predictable, although that climactic bloodbath is well filmed and entertaining.

Music is used very effectively throughout *13 Assassins*, enhancing the story by rumbling away in the background rather than assaulting the viewer with excess decibels. The lighting and sets for the early indoor scenes are stunning. There are elegantly designed interiors, tatami mats, and silk screen landscape paintings in the background; it is all extremely atmospheric and beautiful.

The acting is top class, particularly by the older actors. The cast is a mix of established actors alongside younger generation figures such as Goro Inagaki of popular Japanese boy band SMAP. Inagaki is very convincing as the psychopathic evil lord who thinks nothing of shooting arrows into a tied-up and helpless family, even killing a child in this barbaric manner.

The older actors are superb in *13 Assassins*, particularly Koji Yakusho. He dominates the film, infusing his character with a mix of dignity, anger and humour.

There is no shortage of violence in this film, as is to be expected from director Takashi Miike and the samurai genre. The opening scene shows a lone figure committing seppuku. Although we don't see the blade going into the figure's body, the vivid squelching sounds leave little to the imagination; various organs are heard to plop out the person's body onto the ground before he slumps forward, at which point a long shot shows the body lying in a pool of blood under a grim grey cloudy sky.

One of the highlights of this film is the saké and shamisen scene, in which the samurai warriors get drunk with the geisha girls. The shamisen playing is boisterous and euphoric. It puts me in a shamisen mood, so when I get back home after the film I put on the Yoshida Brothers Prism cd and become entranced by track five, 'Mr Nagano's Foolish Proposal'. That track's ethereal blend of keyboards and shamisen possesses a strange eerie beauty that draws me back to it again and again.

Kantsubaki

Asakusa Meigaza

According to official statistics, the sunniest public holiday in Japan is Culture Day, which is held every 3rd November. And so it turned out earlier this week, when a beautiful autumnal day with blue skies and sunshine drew me and thousands of others to Yoyogi Park to enjoy the leaves that were just beginning to turn red and yellow, the fresh air, and the musicians busking in various parts of the park.

In one area someone was playing a didgeridoo, its undulating drone by chance complemented by a trio of drummers who were playing a short distance further on. Near the Harajuku entrance to the park, a saxophonist blared unmelodically whilst immediately in front of him a woman with a red wig and white powdered face performed some kind of slow motion dance. The saxophone player then stopped playing his instrument and instead started wailing and screaming, with the dancer continuing her slow motion moves, shooting a beady bulgy-eyed glare at the bewildered passers-by.

I gave the demented saxophonist and his dancer a wide berth and headed towards the takoyaki stand by the entrance gate, where I bought some octopus balls to wolf down as a mid-afternoon snack.

Because the guide books all mention Takeshita Dori as a must-see street in Harajuku, I made my way there from Yoyogi Park to check that street out.

Big mistake.

It was hellish. So many people crowded the street that I could hardly move. After a few hundred yards I escaped down a side street and ended up in Omote-sando, where there is a splendid antenna shop selling products from the Niigata region.

These antenna shops can be found dotted around Tokyo, each shop specializing in products from a certain region of Japan. At the Niigata store, I stocked up on some terrific beer from the Echigo craft brewery, a bottle of white wine from the Agricore Echigo Winery in Minami Uonuma, and a bottle of junmai saké from Yoshinogawa Co.Ltd.

Three weeks and some great Niigata-related drinking later, it's now a fine Saturday morning in late November. The weather is bright and sunny. The leaves on the trees are turning red and yellow. As I walk from Azabudai to Roppongi Itchome I kick my way through the crisp dry leaves that are strewn on the pavement, such a satisfying feeling.

The half-litre of saké that I quaffed during the meal last night at Ostrea Oyster Bar & Restaurant in

Roppongi is making me feel slightly bleary. Ostrea in Roppongi is a terrific place to sample oysters from different regions of Japan, as well as a few foreign imports. I hadn't realized how much variation in flavour there is between oysters from different places.

As well as great food, the service in Ostrea was exceptional even by Japan's high standards. As the Friday night went on, the restaurant filled up and became quite boisterous, yet the staff remained good-humoured and attentive as the pace picked up. It was good to see a well run, busy restaurant ticking over so smoothly.

With last night's hangover slowly dissipating, from Roppongi Itchome I take the Namboku Line train to Tameike Sanno. I change there onto the Ginza Line for Asakusa.

At Asakusa metro station I emerge from the Azumabashi exit. The sight that greets me is the famous 'golden turd' on the roof of an office building on the opposite side of the Sumida River. The official city map coyly refers to it as a 'big golden object', but everyone calls it the golden turd because of its unfortunate resemblance to a huge jobby. It's quite a sight.

It is such a beautiful crisp morning that instead of heading straight towards Asakusa Meigaza cinema, I have a wander across the Azumabashi bridge to enjoy the view of the Sumida River under a perfect blue sky. I don't linger too long, though, as I have never been to Asakusa Meigaza before and I want to make sure that I have enough time to locate it before the film starts.

It is no exaggeration to say that Asakusa Meigaza is a legendary cinema in Tokyo. One of the oldest cinemas in the city, it is famous for its downbeat, unpretentious feel.

In terms of a cinema-going experience, Asakusa Meigaza is at the opposite end of the spectrum from the cold corporate multiplexes that dominate today's market. Whereas multiplexes are typically sanitized, characterless, over-branded and family-friendly, Asakusa Meigaza is devoid of advertising, oozes edgy character that some will relish and others won't, and caters to an audience which on my visit today consists entirely of middle-aged men sitting on their own.

There must be around one hundred people in the audience, all of them guys. And no, it isn't a porn film that's showing.

Whilst I certainly wouldn't put Asakusa Meigaza top of my list for bringing someone on a date, the cinema does have its plus points. The seats are reasonably comfortable. You don't have to sit through endless trailers and adverts as none at all are shown before the film. For the price of a 1200-yen ticket you can stay here as long as you like and watch a triple bill of interesting Japanese films that are unlikely to ever be shown outside of Japan.

Asakusa Meigaza is easily recognized from the outside by its red-tiled facade. It is located at the north end of what the local map calls 'Rokku Broadway', a wide street that gets tangibly more sleazy as you head down it from the tourist-trap surroundings of Kaminarimon Dori. There is a porn cinema next to Asakusa Meigaza, and a huge betting complex that looks and feels more like a busy train station than a bookies.

This Saturday morning a couple of down-and-outs are standing in the street clutching their cans of beer, staring at nothing in particular. Other guys, downbeat but less derelict, are checking out the posters outside the cinemas to see what is being shown today.

Kantsubaki is the film I have come to see at Asakusa Meigaza.

Released in 1992 and directed by Yasuo Furuhata, *Kantsubaki* is based on Tomiko Miyao's novel about a young woman called Botan who is sold as a geisha by her gambling addict father. In this new life she is forced into prostitution, a victim of what nowadays would be called human trafficking. The film is set in 1932, the early part of the Showa Era, and the sets are evocative of that period.

Lead actress Yoko Minamino is very good as Botan, whilst Toshiyuki Nishida puts in a terrific performance as Tomita, the man who is responsible for placing Botan as a geisha but who ultimately helps rescue her from that life of exploitation.

The obligatory swordfight bloodbath near the end is done quite entertainingly. After that frenzied scene the film meanders to a serene conclusion. *Kantsubaki* is by no means a classic film and some of the editing is pretty abrupt, as if too much footage was shot and some drastic action had to be taken in the cutting room. But the acting is good and the story is compelling.

I emerge from the bowels of Asakusa Meigaza out into the bright sunshine of this beautiful winter day. Asakusa is such an atmospheric quarter of Tokyo. As I wander around its street restaurants and shotengai arcades, I can feel the spirit of old Edo lingering in the air.

Tokyo's shitamachi soul lives on in Asakusa.

Game of Death

Ginza Cine Pathos

Shimbashi Bunka Cinema doesn't put its listings online, so I go down to salarymanland in person to check out what is showing at this under-the-train-tracks venue.

The choice of films is underwhelming. It is either *Jennifer's Body* or *Prince of Persia – The Sands of Time.* I don't fancy either of them and instead head along by the rail tracks towards Yurakucho, where a more beguiling range of options awaits. Toho Chanter is hosting a Jean-Luc Godard retrospective, whilst Yurakucho Human Trust Cinema is showing what by all accounts is an entertaining Japanese romantic comedy called *Cast Me If You Can.*

But despite those temptations, I can't resist the chance to visit Ginza Cine Pathos, a seductively downbeat earthy cinema that lurks incongruously in its subterranean lair amid the prevailing glitz and glamour of Ginza.

Not much information is available in English about Ginza Cine Pathos. When I used machine translation software to translate a Japanese description of the cinema into English, the following wonderful gibberish came spewing out:

"Basement lined streets, the atmosphere and still remain so Kurosawa Akira movie coming out in 1955, small shop, small café old-fashioned, eaves and other seedy adult shops that. Next to the entrance of the Shinepatosu seems to be able to discover many interesting and a few meters between the public toilets or have a little person."

That is surrealist poetry, with its extraordinary and unexpected juxtapositions of random unconnected concepts and phrases. Placed together the words mean nothing, but somehow they delight the mind.

Ginza Cine Pathos is located underneath Miharabashi Bridge on Harumi-Dori, a couple of minutes walk from Higashi Ginza station. The underpass that houses the cinema is near Bikkuri Sushi Ginza restaurant. The auditorium has comfortable red seats with plenty leg room. Including me, a grand total of four people are in the audience for this Tuesday afternoon showing of the appallingly titled but nonetheless intriguing film, *Game of Death*.

The cinematography by Erik Curtis is stunning. The music is great and perfectly complements the gritty urban backdrop. Wesley Snipes puts in a performance that fluctuates oddly between credible and lackadaisical. In some scenes he seems strangely detached, as if wondering whether he forgot something when he left home. In other scenes he looks more intense and engaged.

Zoe Bell is very good in this film. She exudes star quality, smoothly making the transition from her previous career as stunt double to her new role as star.

The dialogue is a bit iffy and doesn't exactly sparkle, and the film's portentous title fails to inspire confidence. But *Game of Death* turns out to be a surprisingly entertaining film, albeit more for its visual impact than for its script.

Despite what some critics have said, the film is worth a look – provided of course that you set your expectations at a suitably modest level.

After the film I feel in the mood for awamori. So I head across town to Churari Roppongi, where I enjoy a couple of excellent awamoris. The first is Chulajima from a distillery on mainland Okinawa. This one has a light, spearmint fragrance and smooth body. The flavour is grassy and cleansing, the finish short. It is described on the menu as a beginner's awamori. The second awamori, Yonaguni, is more memorable and distinctive. Yonaguni is the southernmost awamori distillery. This awamori has a fresh lemony nose and a big thick body. The flavour is spice and fennel and the long finish delivers a warm afterglow together with a hot kick like whisky. Terrific stuff.

Machete

Wald 9 Cinema Shinjuku

Yamatane Museum of Art's new exhibition has just started. Its full title is 'Establishing Modern Art in Japan: The Artists of the *Nihon Bijutsuin*, from Yokoyama Taikan to Hirayama Ikuo'. The exhibition includes paintings by artists active in the Meiji, Taisho, Showa and Heisei eras.

Hoping that it will be as good as the Yamatane's previous exhibitions this year, I go along and am not disappointed.

Yokoyama Taikan's Showa period pieces 'Mountains in Bright Moonlight' and 'Stream and Autumn Colors' are highly atmospheric, as is Kobayashi Kokei's 'Kumano Shrine'. Many of the other works on display are equally good. I particularly like Okumura Togyu's 'Maelstrom at Naruto', which is especially good when viewed from a distance; the lush, luxuriant, deeply swept greens of Omoda Seiju's 'Hillside Road'; Sakai Sanryo's wonderful 'Cormorant Fishing', showing cormorants and fishing boats in the foreground, the lights of the lamps illuminating the darkness as huge mountains loom in the background; and Goto Sumio's

'Waterfall', in which the flattened perspective of the painting is very effective, particularly on the side of the canvas next to the waterfall, where the forest and rocks spread out tantalizingly.

One of the more modern paintings (from 1981) is Matsuo Toshio's 'Cranes Flying over the Northern Vastness', which is not only a great painting but also a wonderful title. Another painting with a great poetic title is 'Sounds of Wind through Pine Leaves' by Ito Hoji. This painting is very large, one of the biggest in the exhibition. It shows a lone figure sitting on the ground amongst pine trees. That's it. Nothing more. It's powerful, though. The man sitting there in the pines looks solid, literally and spiritually grounded, in a state of harmony with the world akin to that which reiki practitioners seek to achieve.

Amongst all these superb paintings, one stands out. It is Iwahashi Eien's 'Splendor of the Setting Sun', an absolutely stunning picture that glows so much that you feel warm just looking at it. This is one of those paintings that grabs your attention and won't let go. I am not the only person entranced by this magnificent painting. Another visitor can't drag himself away from it, walking right up to it, then taking a few steps back, examining it from all angles.

The only disappointing aspect of the 'Establishing Modern Art in Japan' exhibition is that the museum shop does not have a book to accompany the exhibition. It would have been good to have a permanent reminder of this exceptional exhibition.

Feeling uplifted by the wonderful Yamatane exhibition, I take the train from Ebisu to Shinjuku to go see *Machete* at Wald 9 cinema. When I get to Wald 9 I can't believe it when the person at the box office tells me that the 3.30 p.m. showing of *Machete* is sold out. Usually, the midweek afternoon showings that I go to have only a handful of people in the audience. In stunned disbelief at not being able to get a ticket for the film, I wander out of the cinema and consider my options.

I don't have a Plan B, as I hadn't even contemplated the possibility of the afternoon showing being sold out.

I check out the nearby Musashino cinema but nothing there appeals: *Amelia* with Richard Gere, *Brooklyn's Finest*, and so on. Along at Ikebukuro, Shin-Bungeiza is showing the original 1954 version of *Godzilla* as part of an Ishiro Honda retrospective, which is very tempting. But I probably wouldn't make it there in time for the start of the film.

So I decide to retrace my steps back to Wald 9, where I buy a ticket for the 7.50 p.m. showing of *Machete*. I still don't understand why the mid-afternoon showing is sold out whereas the evening showing, which you would expect to be the busier time, still has tickets available. But never mind, it's just a minor inconvenience, not the end of the world.

Now I am in Shinjuku with plenty of time on my hands before the evening showing of *Machete*. I walk as far as a point near Shinjuku train station from where in one direction I can see the skyscrapers of the Tokyo Metropolitan Government district oozing political power, whilst if I turn my gaze in the opposite direction the bright brash neon sleaze of Kabukicho assails me.

Irish pub Dubliners beckons. I drop in for a couple of pints of Kilkenny. Today the price of all drinks is reduced to 500 yen as it is the bar's anniversary, so my unplanned visit here on this day is a lucky piece of timing.

After the liquid refreshment it is time for some food. I head over to Numazukou, a conveyor belt sushi joint in the bowels of Shinjuku Station. It's a great place. Normally I'm not a fan of brightly lit restaurants, but Numazukou has a good lively atmosphere despite its bright lighting. The clientele when I get here consists of a mix of salarymen dropping in for sushi and a beer after their day's work, a couple of families, and one or two stray foreigners like me. Shouts constantly ring out from the waiting staff, either shouting orders to the chefs or shouting greetings to newly arrived customers.

The sushi is delicious. I wash it down with a bottle of dry saké from Shizuoka prefecture.

A conveyor belt is such a great way to present sushi. Tempting dishes continually pass by just inches before your eyes. It is so easy to reach out and grab whatever you like the look of.

The place soon fills up and several people are waiting by the entrance to be seated. Sushi restaurant etiquette dictates that you don't hang around once you have finished eating, particularly when others are waiting to be seated. So, well fed and watered, I set off back to Wald 9.

After two pints of Kilkenny and a bottle of Shizuoka sake, I am in a perfect mood to enjoy *Machete.*

The film is showing in Screen 7, a cosy 81-seater. My seat is D1, a very well placed seat on the left hand side of the auditorium quite near the screen. The only problem with this seat is that I am trapped next to the wall with no means of escape when the final credits roll. At the end of a film in most Tokyo cinemas, not a single person gets up to leave until the entire credits have finished. I don't fancy clambering clumsily over everyone else in my row to get out, so I will be stuck when today's film ends. It doesn't really matter, though, as I'm in no particular hurry to get anywhere after the film.

Machete is violent, sexy and funny. Its star-studded cast and tongue-in-cheek bravado make this film a highly entertaining spectacle. Although it has a serious subject matter – illegal immigration into the United States from Mexico – the film entertains rather than pontificates, albeit its liberal political stance is never far from the surface.

It is quite an achievement to have assembled a cast that includes Robert De Niro, Jessica Alba, Michelle

Rodriguez, Steven Seagal, Don Johnson, Jeff Fahey, and Lindsay Lohan. But the undoubted star of the show is Danny Trejo, who plays the Machete of the title.

Danny Trejo exudes menace. His intimidating face and withering glare leave you in no doubt that this is not a man to be messed with. Even though he is in stellar company in such a cast, he carries off his leading role with great style and charisma.

The Japanese subtitler didn't bother translating one of the great throwaway lines in this darkly humourous romp of a film. When De Niro's character, a slimy racist Senator, is about to go into a press conference, his assistant gives him his walking stick and tells him to try and make the assembled journalists feel sorry for him. In that scene, De Niro's character is trying to win the sympathy vote on the basis of a gunshot wound that he himself orchestrated. It would have been interesting to see the Japanese translation of that line. But no translation is given in the subtitles and so, being the only non-Japanese person in the audience, I am the only person who laughs.

The King of Kings

Cinema Vera Shibuya

As I'm taking a leisurely ride on one of the exercise bikes at the gym this morning, there is one guy using a machine in front of me which I have never used. The machine seems to replicate the experience of cross-country skiing. The man using it looks like he is in his mid-thirties. He has a shaved head, a smartphone belted onto his arm, and the Wall Street Journal spread open before him balanced on the frame of the machine.

He is sprinting furiously on the machine, listening to something on his smartphone, and reading his newspaper all at the same time; a prodigious multi-tasker, expending far too much pointless effort in my view.

Whilst I am hanging around waiting to meet someone outside the gym afterwards, that same guy appears. He comes jogging out of the gym on the way to his next engagement, phone clamped to his ear. Does he never rest?

As this is my last visit to the gym before leaving Tokyo at the end of my three-year stay in this wonderful city, I hand in my locker keys at the front desk. I also retrieve my squash racket from under the thick layer of dust that has accumulated upon it during the previous months of non-use. All I have made use of in the gym are the weights and the exercise bikes; I haven't played squash for over half a year.

As I walk along Meiji Dori towards Shibuya, I feel quite melancholy about this being the last time I will have gone to the gym. The gym has become a regular feature of my life. It's strange how you can get attached to such things. I even felt the same way about my last visit to the dentist earlier in the week.

In Shibuya my destination is Cinema Vera. This cinema shares a building with Eurospace cinema, where a few weeks ago I saw the wonderful black and white documentary *Koyamaru*. Their decor is so similar that it is hard to discern why Cinema Vera and Eurospace exist as separate entities: both have a programming policy that features interesting non-mainstream films, they share the same building, and their design is almost identical.

The auditorium at Cinema Vera has an almost academic, lecture hall feel. But it seems to have a bit more leg room than the Eurospace auditorium downstairs on a lower floor of the building, which makes watching today's offering, Cecil B. DeMille's 1927 silent film *The King of Kings*, a slightly more comfortable experience than watching *Koyamaru* was.

The King of Kings is showing as part of what looks like a marvellous two weeks of silent movies running at Cinema Vera during December. This sixty-five minute version of *The King of Kings* provides a brisk retelling of the story of Jesus' crucifixion. The original film was nearly two hours long, so this is a severely truncated version that is being shown today.

It's a strange feeling to be sitting amongst a cinema audience watching a film that is completely silent. There is no spoken dialogue and no musical accompaniment. The utter silence creates an intensity that you do not get with modern films, in which silence is used only sporadically.

One of the most striking characteristics of silent films is the bulging-eyes style of acting that the actors use. Presumably this exaggerated style is used in order to compensate for the lack of spoken dialogue in the pre-sound days of the film industry. It's a hammy style of acting that has widely fallen out of fashion, although it is still very much in vogue amongst the no-talent *tarentos* who infest Japanese television programmes.

The male lead H.B. Warner seems a bit old to be playing the role of Jesus. You would expect someone at least a couple of decades younger to have been cast in that role. But he carries it off well, helped by the glowing light in which he is bathed in his scenes.

Joseph Schildkraut plays Judas Iscariot very well, powerfully projecting the character's humanity, weakness and guilt.

The climax of the film is a trademark Cecil B. DeMille spectacle. As Jesus hangs on the cross, the sky clouds over, wind begins to howl, lightning strikes and the earth shakes and splits, swallowing up the body of Judas that is seen hanging from a tree. The extras look suitably terrified as they stampede to escape from the prevailing pandemonium.

The print for today's film is very scratchy. But as with many of these old films, that scratchiness adds to the charm. At the end of the film about half of the twenty or so people in the audience get up and leave, whilst the other half stay in their seats waiting for the next film.

I get up and leave and head towards the Shibuya Tower Records store a few minutes walk away to get a cd by Jake Shimabukuro, the phenomenally talented ukulele player. The ukulele may have a naff image but in the hands of Jake Shimabukuro, it is a magical instrument.

I first heard Shimabukuro while I was having a therapeutic massage for a back problem that had rendered me almost immobile. Some great background music was playing during the massage. I asked what it was, and then back home I checked out some videos of Shimabukuro on YouTube. The one that really grabbed me was 'Bluegrass Ukulele', one of the most amazing demonstrations of virtuosity I have ever seen, particularly during the spectacular final minute.

On the My Life compilation that I buy at the Shibuya store, Jake Shimabukuro does a cover of Jimmy Page and Robert Plant's 'Going to California' that is so good that I play it five or six times in a row back at my apartment in Azabudai. If anyone can make the ukulele cool, it is Shimabukuro-san.

Norwegian Wood

Kadokawa Cineplex Mito

Nobody I know has been raving about director Anh Hung Tran's film version of the Haruki Murakami novel *Norwegian Wood* and having just sat through it, I can see why. About three-quarters of the way through the film, someone sitting in the row behind me lets out a big sigh. That sound of bored exasperation sums up the feeling of ennui brought on by this disappointing film.

As a big fan of Haruki Murakami's writing, it's hard not to feel irked at this film's lacklustre rendering of one of the great novels in world literature.

Despite the negative reviews that the film has received, I go to see it clinging to the hope that it will be better than the reviews make it out to be. But my heart sinks immediately as the opening scenes jerk by in staccato fashion. Each of the early scenes feels truncated, as if the film makers are in a hurry to get past the Kizuki portion of the story as fast as they can. This does not bode well and sure enough, the rest of the film proves to be as disappointing as those opening scenes.

In *Norwegian Wood*, lead actress Rinko Kikuchi (playing Naoko) swaps her usual brooding style for two affectations: exaggerated rapid eye movement to denote her character's mental instability, and an extremely irritating baby-voice. The irony is that Kikuchi's usual brooding style would have been much more suited to the role that she plays in this film, rather than the child-like personification with which she imbues the Naoko character.

Rinko Kikuchi is a very good actress. If she had chosen to play it differently, she could have given a great performance in this role.

Everything that happens in this film is presented in a stagey manner. Toru and Naoko out in the mountains, Naoko striding from right to left, then left to right, then back again with Toru tagging along behind; and the scene in Midori's house where the characters ponderously weave their way from one room to another. Towards the end of the film, the glowing woolly scarves and hats make the actors look like models in a Uniqlo advert.

The mewling soundtrack reinforces the one-note atmosphere of the film. Murakami's wonderful novel is richly layered in joy, restlessness, grief, introspection, love, humour, nostalgia, and the thrill of sex. But you wouldn't know that from this dull film version.

Ken'ichi Matsuyama, who plays Toru Watanabe, could have been very good in this role but the script gives him little opportunity to do justice to it.

Matsuyama's performance is a convincingly faithful embodiment of the character from the book.

The other two members of the cast who rise above the prevailing mediocrity of the film are Eriko Hatsune, who is superb as Hatsumi, and Tetsuji Tamayama, who is equally good as the suave and worldly yet utterly callous Nagasawa. Unfortunately, Hatsune and Tamayama don't get much screen time.

In her scenes, Hatsune exudes charisma, class, and hidden vulnerability. She commands the screen, perfectly capturing the pride and fragility of the Hatsumi character in the book. Her electrifying though brief appearance is the high point of the film.

Whatever Works

Ebisu Garden Place Cinema

Summers in Tokyo are hot, humid and physically draining. Winters, on the other hand, are wonderful. December days like today lift your spirits with their bright sun, cool freshness and perfect blue skies.

Ebisu is one of the best areas of Tokyo to enjoy such days. I head here today to see my last film in Tokyo, Woody Allen's *Whatever Works*, which is showing at Ebisu Garden Place Cinema.

I arrive early at the cinema. After buying my ticket for the film, I walk over to the nearby Tokyo Metropolitan Museum of Photography to check out their current exhibition, 'Contemporary Japanese Photography, vol. 9 – The New Snapshot'. The best works on display are by Nakamura Haruko and Obata Yuji. Nakamura's photographs are characterized by strikingly vibrant colours that exude an infectious joie de vivre. The impact of this is poignantly heightened when you learn from the exhibition notes that Nakamura died prematurely in 2005 while in her forties.

The other outstanding pictures in this exhibition are by Obata Yuji, whose superb photographs of

Hokkaido winter scenes feature kids skating, a railway station under snow, and evening traffic in the far north midwinter cold. There are also some amazingly sharp and vivid close-up pictures of falling snowflakes, demonstrating Obata's mastery of macro as well as landscape techniques.

Back at the cinema, a surprisingly large audience has gathered for the Friday afternoon showing of *Whatever Works*. I was expecting to have the auditorium almost to myself, but a substantial, diverse audience are in their seats well before the film starts.

The film is directed by Woody Allen and stars Larry David. For fans of sharp and cynical New York humour, the Woody Allen/Larry David combo is absolutely mouthwatering.

Larry David plays the role of Boris, an emotionally stunted misanthropic intellectual. This is the role that Woody Allen would normally allocate to himself, but Larry David carries it off magnificently. As the film proceeds, it is easy to visualize Woody Allen in the Larry David role. But Larry David brings an extra notch of rage to the role that you would not get from the more mild-mannered Allen.

Things sizzle right from the opening scene, which climaxes with Larry David delivering a brilliant monologue direct to camera. In this way, the audience is immediately drawn into the action.

With its lampooning of Deep South religious conservatives, this film won't do much business in the

Bible Belt. But of course that is not the target market for *Whatever Works*. This film is for people who love *Seinfeld*, *Curb Your Enthusiasm* and Woody Allen's back catalogue.

The dialogue is vintage Woody Allen. He wrote the script back in the 1970s but it is only now that it has been turned into a film. The original script is brought up to date with a couple of topical references, although the core theme of the script is timeless, namely, how can we live in a world that is so full of horror, bigotry, violence, small-mindedness and injustice? The two words of the film title may appear to be a somewhat feeble response to this conundrum, but as it turns out, the script is eloquent and profound as well as being extremely funny.

Nobody but Woody Allen is capable of discussing existential angst with such an intoxicating blend of good humour and misanthropic delight.

Patricia Clarkson provides a wonderful contribution to *Whatever Works*. She plays the part of Marietta, the bible-bashing mother of the young woman who has shacked up with Boris in his New York apartment. Patricia Clarkson will be known to *Frasier* fans for her guest role as Frasier's girlfriend in a few episodes of that series, including the episode where Frasier and her go for a fraught holiday to the Caribbean together with Niles and Daphne and Martin Crane, the father of the Crane boys.

In *Whatever Works*, Clarkson's character undergoes a radical transformation from alcoholic religious nut to avant-garde conceptual artist. When her ex-husband shows up in New York City from Mississipi, he undergoes an equally funny if implausible transformation.

At one point in the film, Larry David speaks directly to the audience and states bluntly that this is not a feelgood movie. How untrue that is! Contrary to Larry David's assertion, *Whatever Works* is the ultimate feelgood movie. It confronts the hideousness, stupidity and cruelty of much human behaviour, yet emerges with a host of life-affirming laughs.

Whatever Works is vintage Woody Allen, classic Larry David, and one of the funniest films I have ever seen. As I walk back home from Ebisu to Azabudai after the film, I can barely keep a grin off my face.

LONDON

The Big Picture

Curzon Renoir

Sunday morning turns out to be a good time to visit the National Gallery on Trafalgar Square. Although there are plenty people here, it isn't too busy and I can get more or less clear views of the paintings on display. With the increasing popularity of blockbuster art exhibitions, some people have given up on visiting famous galleries because of the mobbed spaces and having to jostle for snatched views of the most popular exhibits.

So I'm lucky today, as I get clear unimpeded views even of tourist-magnet paintings such as Van Gogh's 'Sunflowers' (1888) and Degas' 'Miss La La at the Cirque Fernando' (1879). The sparse crowds helpfully part at convenient moments to give me panoramic views from the other side of the room over to Van Gogh's famous picture. Also with other pictures it is possible to view them from different angles, at least for a few seconds, without other visitors getting in the way.

The National Gallery building itself is stunning, with its beautifully tiled floors at the entrance and its wonderful exhibition rooms. Like almost everyone else,

I bypass the thirteenth-century to seventeenth-century collections and make straight for the impressionists.

Normally I would avoid such sheep-like behaviour, but the lure of this gallery's impressionist collection is irresistible. It's strange how impressionist painting has, more than any other style, morphed into a slick twenty-first century marketing operation. Monet, Manet, Degas, Renoir, Gauguin, Cézanne… all can be found in the gallery shop in whatever product form you could ever want – tablemats, calendars, umbrellas, bags, fridge magnets, coffee mugs, and on and on.

But even this rampant commercialism can't overshadow the brilliance of the paintings. It is amazing to be in the presence of so much great art in one place.

Two paintings by Camille Pissarro displayed side by side highlight that artist's genius. On the left is 'The Boulevard Montmartre at Night' (1897). On the right is 'The Louvre under Snow' (1902), a beautiful snowy Paris scene. The 'Boulevard Montmartre' picture is Pissarro's only night-time picture. It's hard to believe that he painted only one night picture in his whole career, given how great that one picture is. The diagonal composition of the picture leads your eye to the deep purple evening sky where the boulevard meets the horizon, the dynamic night sky radiating over street traffic and blurry foreground figures walking on each side of the boulevard.

The standout picture for me, amongst the French collection, is Jean-Baptiste-Camille Corot's superb

'Avignon from the West' (1836). Corot is one of the great French landscape artists. There is a breezy freshness to this Avignon painting that makes it invigorating to look at. The composition is simple but perfectly balanced, and the palette of subdued blues and greens has a quiet, soothing, but nevertheless strong effect.

Only a few paces away from Corot, the National Gallery has some great English landscape pictures by the big two of that era, Constable and Turner. Turner's picture 'The Fighting Temeraire' (1839) lives up to its iconic status, a superb majestic rendering of the old warship being towed by a tugboat along the River Thames to Rotherhithe, where it is to be broken up at the end of its illustrious career. Turner's magnificent sunset sky conveys the melancholy of the quietly epic scene.

His other paintings demonstrate Turner's considerable stylistic range, from the minutely detailed elemental chaos of 'Calais Pier, with French Poissards Preparing for Sea: an English Packet Arriving' (1803) to the vague abstract blur of 'Rain, Steam, and Speed – the Great Western Railway' (1844). Turner often used big canvases and these enhance the dramatic effect of his pictures.

It's great to see Constable's large canvases in person here today. I had seen reproductions of 'The Haywain' (1821) before, but the picture had seemed to me bucolic and dull. However, when you stand in front of 'The Haywain' and view it in person, the painting glows with energy and beauty; the sunlight sparkles on the river surface in an understated yet vivid way, and the cloud-shadows over the open fields brilliantly conjure up an English summer day.

Another of Constable's paintings, 'The Cornfield' (1826), exerts a similar effect. When seen reduced to fit the size of a computer screen or a book page, this picture looks pleasant but forgettable. But when you see it in person here at the National Gallery, it has the same dynamism and splendour as 'The Haywain'.

The other Constable picture that leaves an enduring impression is 'Weymouth Bay' (1816), an almost deserted coastal landscape with bold dabs of paint giving the cloudscape a solidity and permanence quite unlike the more naturalistic clouds in 'The Cornfield'.

You can only take in so much during a single visit to a gallery the size of the National in London, so the older collections will have to wait for a future visit.

Sated with the impressionist riches and the Turner and Constable masterpieces, I head back out into the sunshine and enjoy a great long lunch at Maison Touareg, a Moroccan and Lebanese restaurant on Greek Street in Soho. Thick and delicious lentil soup is followed by wonderful lamb couscous and mezes, washed down with a bottle of crisp refreshing Lebanese white wine.

From Greek Street it doesn't take long to walk to Renoir Cinema near Russell Square. Part of the Curzon group, there is always an interesting programme at this cinema. The film I've come to see today is *The Big*

Picture, a French film based on the book of that name by American author Douglas Kennedy. In French, the film is titled *L'Homme qui Voulait Vivre Sa Vie*, which translates as 'The Man who Wanted to Live His Life'.

The Big Picture has received some positive reviews from British critics, though the film isn't particularly memorable.

It's being shown in Screen 2 of the Renoir Cinema. Screen 2 is a comfortable enough auditorium. But the lights don't go fully down during the film, which takes something away from the intensity of the viewing experience. The forthcoming refurbishment of the cinema may change that.

The Big Picture is uneven, a hotchpotch of a film consisting of three distinct sections. The first is the breakdown of the hero's marriage, which is done convincingly. The second is the hero's accidental murder of the smug man who has been having an affair with the hero's wife, the disposal of said corpse, and the hero's escape to a far-flung corner of Europe where he attempts to carve out a life of discreet anonymity. The third part shows the new life that the hero gradually builds as a photographer, a profession which had been his unrealized life dream before he got suffocated by a life of domestic responsibilities.

The first part of the film is done well.

The second part sags badly.

The third part picks up the pace and has some entertaining passages, which are however marred by some preposterous plot development that overwhelms my willingness to suspend disbelief. The hero, for example, gets thrown overboard from a large ship into a dark and choppy sea, but survives unfeasibly easily. It's hard to empathize with a character who is scripted as invincible and indestructible rather than humanly vulnerable.

A good cast does what it can with the limited material at its disposal. Romain Duris is very good in the lead role, confronting his frustrations with a quiet intensity before making his break for freedom. Marina Foïs puts in a good performance as his wife, an unsympathetic character who is portrayed, fairly or otherwise, as the villain of the piece in their disintegrating marriage.

The true touch of class in the film is provided by French screen legend Catherine Deneuve, although her role is a limited one.

The dialogue, particularly between the husband and wife in the first part of the film, is punchy and very American. It has none of the elegance that you might hope for if it had been an original French script rather than a translation based on an American book.

Although there is some mildly appealing existential meandering in the latter part of the film, the forthright source keeps showing through: the film is more Sarkozy than Mitterrand.

The Woman in the Fifth

Curzon Soho

Earlier today it has been grey and wet. But by mid-evening, when we venture out, London has that fresh after-the-rain feel. There isn't much time for a meal before the film so we look for somewhere that will be quick and relatively cheap. Golden Day restaurant opposite Curzon Soho cinema seems to fit the bill, so in we go.

The seafood noodles are excellent, washed down with a Tsingtao beer. There is nothing fancy about this restaurant but it's perfect for a quick and tasty pre-film meal.

After wolfing down the meal at Golden Day, we cross over Shaftesbury Avenue to Curzon Soho cinema. At the box office, when I pick up the tickets I had ordered online I notice that specific seat numbers have been assigned, even though the online booking process did not offer a choice of where to sit; nor did it even mention that specific seats would be assigned. Because I had ordered the two tickets on separate occasions, the seats we have been allocated are not next to each other.

I ask the box office person to change the tickets. She is helpful enough, though she says that she will have to summon a manager to authorize the seat changes. A manager duly appears and sanctions the seat change. The ticket printouts should have been for seats J11 and J12, but the J11 ticket refuses to print out. So the manager prints out two tickets with J12 on them and then manually scribbles a change to make one of them J11. A bit of a rigmarole but it doesn't take too long to get it sorted.

On this Saturday evening the cinema is buzzing. The mezzanine bar is doing a brisk trade. There are plenty people hanging out here and also in the space lower down in front of the auditoriums; it's a good lively vibe.

The film we have come to see, *The Woman in the Fifth*, is showing in Screen 2, a very good auditorium decked out in vivid blue. The seats are comfortable, although I won't sit in row J again as there isn't as much leg room there as in the rows nearer the screen.

What a great film *The Woman in the Fifth* turns out to be. Having seen the underwhelming trailer, my expectations were modest. But this film turns out to be surprisingly brilliant. There is great use of music to create a subtle sense of unease. Many scenes are shot in bright sunlight, and this sets up a very effective dissonance between the happy summery visual impact of the outdoor scenes and the dark psychological turmoil simmering below the surface.

Ethan Hawke is excellent as Tom Ricks, the frazzled yet far from totally defeated anti-hero. Kristin Scott Thomas is beguiling as Margit, the literary muse for Hawke's character. Samir Guesmi is terrific as the café owner, his deadpan delivery a fine counterpoint to the more anguished Hawke.

The Paris backdrops are de-glamourized for the most part. However, there is one scene – the literary party at which Tom meets the mysterious Margit – in which the Eiffel Tower looms large in its full clichéd splendour. Uh-oh, I thought, they have copped out and resorted to Parisian cliché.

But by the time the film reaches its disturbing dénouement, I have changed my mind. Rather than simply using the Eiffel Tower as a postcard backdrop, I think that director Pawel Pawlikowski is saying look, this is a figment of Tom's imagination, a symptom of his troubled psychological state. Maybe the literary party never even happened; it could instead have been merely a projection of Tom's desire for how his life *should* have turned out rather than how it actually did turn out.

An Italian Straw Hat

Barbican Cinema

With this being a Sunday, Smithfield Market isn't trading today. But you can still walk through the impressive central passageway, its elegant ironwork painted in vivid pink and purple, the dramatic bright colours like those of Hockney's recent landscapes. It would be good to return here early on a weekday morning when the market is in full flow, though even when empty this place has a lot of character and atmosphere.

A minute away from Smithfield Market there is a memorial to Scottish patriot William Wallace, who met his gruesome end here in August 1305 when he was hanged, drawn and quartered. The memorial is discreet and understated. I was expecting something more prominent, given the historical significance of the spot. But I suppose it's natural for Wallace to be celebrated more in his native land of Scotland than down here in the heart of London, England.

For an early lunch I venture into the Rising Sun, an old-fashioned pub located on a corner site with a couple of attractive white-brick floors above it. The landlady is friendly, and the Beef Stout Pudding I have is pretty good. But I don't linger long because at a nearby table there is a loudmouth holding court, the kind of person who wants the whole place to be his audience. So I quickly pay the bill and set off along Long Lane to the Barbican cinema.

The Barbican's appearance certainly lives up to its negative reputation. What a hideous building. Its brutalist architecture is repellent and once you are inside, it's very hard to find your way around. Just as I am beginning to curse the place, a helpful employee notices that I am looking lost. He kindly points out how to get to Cinema 1 when I tell him that that's what I am looking for. This encounter softens my hostility to this unappealing place; the employee is helpful and friendly, a welcome antidote to the bleak ugliness of the building.

When I eventually find Cinema 1, my mood continues to mellow as that auditorium is superb. Its comfortable seats, the steep sloping that ensures a good view no matter what giant or big-haired person sits in front of you, and the pervasive classy atmosphere combine to dissolve the stress of struggling through the rest of the building complex to get here.

I settle into seat F25 to enjoy René Clair's 1927 silent film *An Italian Straw Hat*, with live musical accompaniment by Andrew Youdell on piano.

The film turns out to be absolutely superb. René Clair's direction keeps the story moving along smoothly, with no dull sagging phases that you get when a film is in the hands of a lesser talent. All the cast are great, especially Albert Préjean in the lead role of Ferdinand, the groom. Préjean has a subtly commanding presence. He almost dances his way through this performance, always witty, always sparkling.

An Italian Straw Hat is a comedy of manners. It's delivered with a smattering of slapstick but mainly achieves its effect through the intensely detailed observations of individual behaviour.

The film is entrancing. It is very funny, replete with laugh-out-loud moments. Andrew Youdell's live piano accompaniment is exquisite and contributes hugely to the film experience. When the film ends, there is delighted applause from the audience. A great film, in a great cinema, with great musical accompaniment. I feel privileged to have been here to see it.

There is something magical about these classic old silent films. The style of acting is utterly different from today, the lack of sound technology back then forcing the performers to communicate emotions through marvellously vivid facial expressions rather than through spoken dialogue.

Feeling exhilarated after the film, I manage to extricate myself from the Barbican's brutalist embrace. Outside, I walk briskly to Mabel's Tavern, a good traditional pub just off Euston Road. I'd arranged to meet a friend here who I hadn't seen for a while. We start off with a pint each of Spitfire, an English pale ale that is decent enough but not quite good enough to merit a second pint. We move on to Kent's Best, a refreshing English bitter that is much more inspiring, so we have three pints of that one before calling it a night.

A Dangerous Method

Everyman Screen on The Green, Islington

Today's Freud-fest kicks off with a morning visit to the Lucian Freud 'Portraits' exhibition at the National Portrait Gallery, followed in the afternoon with a showing of the film *A Dangerous Method*, in which one of the main characters is Lucian Freud's famous grandfather Sigmund. A 1938 photograph in the Lucian Freud exhibition book shows a foppish young Lucian and an egghead Sigmund standing together. It seems strange that such a historically significant picture is hidden away at the back of the exhibition book, rather than featuring more prominently.

When I get there, the National Portrait Gallery is busy but not too mobbed. There is a steady flow, rather than a raging torrent, of visitors heading into the gallery through the Charing Cross Road entrance.

The Lucian Freud exhibition covers seven decades of his portraits, from the 1940s up till his death in 2011. It is a stunning exhibition.

Not everything appeals, though. I don't care for the raw brutality of Freud's sprawling nudes. These pictures make up a significant chunk of the overall exhibition. They have a merciless quality that is quite chilling.

I much prefer the other portraits, the non-nudes, in particular the paintings of his first wife, Kitty Garman, in 'Girl with Roses' (1947-8), 'Girl with a Kitten' (1947), and 'Girl in a Dark Jacket' (1947). The latter picture adorns the front cover of the exhibition book. The girl's amazing outsized glassy eyes exert a hypnotic effect on the viewer.

Other great pictures include the creepily powerful 'Hotel Bedroom' (1954) with its stony expression of a relationship that has died; the almost playful 'Red-Haired Man on a Chair' (1962-3), where the sitter perches not entirely comfortably on a chair, the picture given an extra dash of warmth by the beautiful reddish-brown horizontal brush strokes that constitute the background; the Frasier-esque immense forehead in 'Frank Auerbach' (1975-6); 'Esther' (1982-3), a simple yet moving portrait of a woman's head resting on a pillow as she gazes meditatively into the distance, an unusually tender picture in this often hard-edged exhibition; 'Woman with Eyes Closed' (2002), another relatively gentle portrait in which the subject retains a privacy and mystery rather than being explicitly revealed; the steady gaze and relaxed poise of art historian and critic Martin Gayford in 'Man in a Blue Scarf' (2004); and 'David Hockney' (2002), a terrific portrait that perfectly captures Hockney's gruff humanity.

As well as pictures of his family and friends, Freud also painted several self-portraits which give an insight into his self-perception. There is a cheeky humour in 'Interior with Plant, Reflection Listening (Self-Portrait)' (1967-8), a self-portrait in which Freud lurks in the background so unobtrusively that a casual viewer might not even notice him; a supercilious, judgemental glare in 'Reflection (Self-Portrait)' (1981-2); a quiet, less aggressive self-assuredness and self-acceptance in 'Reflection (Self-Portrait)' (1985); and a humble self-effacing air in 'Self-Portrait, Reflection' (2002).

After the exhibition, I walk towards King's Cross. From there, I continue up the long steady incline of Pentonville Road as far as Angel, turning left there onto Upper Street until I get to today's cinema, Islington's wonderful Screen on The Green.

This single-screen cinema must be a strong contender for the title of best cinema in London. It is exactly how a great cinema should be, the antithesis of the bland corporate multiplexes that dominate today's towns and cities.

The Screen on The Green looks great from the outside, and is even better inside. It started life as a cinema in 1913 and has been running almost continuously since then. It oozes character. I almost gasp with pleasure when I enter the auditorium. Not only does it have a superb barrel vault ceiling, luxuriously comfortable red velvet seats, a very good screen and excellent sound system, it also has a full-size bar at the back of the auditorium. What more could you want? You order your drinks at the bar and they bring them to your seat.

This cinema itself is such a pleasurable indulgence, the particular film you have come to see seems almost inconsequential.

I would have been happy to simply sit back and gaze around the auditorium for a while longer, but the film has to start so down go the lights and *A Dangerous Method* gets under way. With one of the main themes of this film being the relationship between Sigmund Freud and Carl Jung, there is a risk of the film getting mired in stiff dry intellectualism. Or cheesy costume drama cliché.

But David Cronenberg is no fool and under his assured direction things move along at a brisk pace, blending personal drama with some cerebral forays into the early days of psychoanalysis.

Keira Knightley has drawn some criticism for her performance as Sabina Spielrein, with accusations of over-acting being directed at her. But that seems unfair. How is she expected to portray a hysterical, deeply troubled patient without showing the unhinged extreme behavior that such people display?

It's not easy to watch her character in such a troubled state. But it's not meant to be easy. It is probably the kind of deranged performance that all acting students have to put on at some point during their days at acting school, but Keira Knightley does it very well in this film and deserves credit for a performance that is well out of her, or anyone else's, comfort zone.

As Sigmund Freud, Viggo Mortensen plays things with just the right blend of intensity and wry detachment. Michael Fassbender is equally good as Carl Jung. The master-disciple relationship between Freud and Jung plays itself out very engagingly, helped along by some beautifully scenic backdrops.

But it's Keira Knightley who is the star of this show. Her role is by far the most challenging of her career to date, and by stepping up so boldly she has opened up infinite possibilities for other powerful roles for herself in the future.

The film finishes around 6 p.m. I had arranged to meet a couple of friends at 7 p.m. in the lobby of the Tavistock Hotel in Bloomsbury, so I have to walk at a brisk pace back past King's Cross to Bloomsbury. Once assembled at the Tavistock, we decide to go for a drink at the Marlborough Arms, a lively old-fashioned London pub nearby where we sink a few pints of London Pride, a very good pale ale, and Young's Gold, a refreshing bitter. It's a good end to the day.

Tinker Tailor Soldier Spy

Odeon Leicester Square Mezzanine

Leicester Square is a building site when I get here today. Fenced off from the public, the main part of the square is taken over by bulldozers and workers busy renovating this London hub. It makes me wonder if the film at the adjacent Odeon Leicester Square cinema will be audible over the din of drills and other mechanical equipment.

Tinker Tailor Soldier Spy is not showing on Odeon Leicester Square's magnificent big screen, but on little Screen 4 in the mezzanine next to the main cinema. It's an uninspiring auditorium. Yet in a perverse way, the drab environment of Screen 4 perfectly matches the bleak, washed out, dreary tones of *Tinker Tailor Soldier Spy*. It feels like the auditorium forms an extension of the melancholy film set.

Though visually drab in terms of the subdued colours on screen, the film is excellent. It is probably too downbeat to draw the multiplex popcorn masses in huge numbers, but that's no bad thing. In fact, the sedate pace and leisurely characterization that imbue this film are a refreshing change from the attention-span-of-a-gnat staccato editing and frenzied action of most contemporary thrillers.

The cast have rightly been praised for their performances. But a huge amount of the credit for the way in which this film turned out is due to director Tomas Alfredson. He never rushes things. Instead, he builds atmosphere by allowing the camera to linger on faces or inanimate objects.

Great credit is also due to cinematographer Hoyte van Hostema for his ability to make dreary grey, brown and sepia aesthetically pleasing rather than depressingly dull.

Gary Oldman deserves the praise he has received for his performance as the quietly intense veteran spy George Smiley. Toby Jones and Colin Firth are both very good as senior figures in the upper echelons of British intelligence. Their allegiances are murky. And it is good to see Kathy Burke popping up in a great little cameo as Connie Sachs. She injects some energy and bawdiness into an otherwise staid yet engrossing spectacle.

I enjoy *Tinker Tailor Soldier Spy*. It is downbeat but gripping. It will be good if a few more film adaptations like this, with substance and polish, are made of other John le Carré spy stories.

From the cinema on Leicester Square, I head to The Lady Ottoline in Bloomsbury for dinner. The Lady Ottoline is often referred to as a 'gastropub' but I find that word repellent and refuse to use it. 'Gastropub' has echoes of gastroenteritis; not an association to stir the appetite.

'Victorian Pub' is another moniker for The Lady Ottoline and whilst that is an improvement on gastropub, it still doesn't convey all that the venue has to offer. Downstairs it does have a pub feel. But upstairs it is a very good restaurant, and it is up the steep wooden stairs that we go tonight for what turns out to be a wonderful meal.

The waitress is friendly and attentive, the atmosphere relaxed and informal, the food terrific. We have starters of mixed beetroot served with Bosworth Ash goat's cheese mousse, and chicken and rabbit terrine wrapped in savoy cabbage with balsamic and port reduction; main courses of pink roasted rump of Blackface lamb, celeriac purée, crispy potatoes, poached fig, thyme jus, and Chart Farm venison loin, celeriac mash, sautéed salsify, wild mushrooms, red currant jelly; and desserts of sticky toffee pudding with butter scotch sauce, and rhubarb crumble with custard.

What a great meal. There is definitely an artist at work in the kitchen.

Extremely Loud & Incredibly Close

Everyman Baker Street

Burlington House, sitting regally on Piccadilly in the heart of London, is a suitably grand setting for the 'David Hockney: A Bigger Picture' exhibition hosted by the Royal Academy of Arts. Since the death last year of Lucian Freud, the media here has not hesitated to crown Hockney as Britain's greatest living artist.

A huge and unrelenting publicity campaign has ensured that this Hockney exhibition is attracting staggering numbers of visitors.

I grew up in York in the north of England and I regularly used to go cycling in the Wolds, the area of East Yorkshire that features heavily in the Hockney exhibition. Sometimes I would cycle from York through Stamford Bridge and on towards Garrowby. Other times I would load my bike onto the Scarborough Line train and get off at Malton and cycle from there. You would almost never see any tourists. Maybe that will change following the mass publicity for this Hockney exhibition.

So, being familiar with the area, I'm intrigued by how Hockney would represent this unspectacular, quietly beautiful part of the world. The Wolds are an area of gentle hills and prime agricultural land. It is not an area suited to coach tours zipping from one iconic sight to another, disgorging camera-clicking tourists.

The queue outside Burlington House is already quite lengthy by the time we get here, twenty minutes before opening time. But it is worth the wait. The immense scale and vibrant colours of the Hockney landscapes in this exhibition are stunning.

A few snotty art critics have turned their noses up at this Hockney exhibition ("Landscapes – how passé!"), but I think that's just the hissy fit of an intellectual elite who have been bypassed by the popularity of Hockney's landscapes and the fact that these superb paintings do not need any patronizing interpretation by self-appointed art experts. This exhibition we get it, we don't need an expert's ponderous erudition to explain it to us.

Before getting to the Yorkshire landscapes, it is good to see his California picture 'Pearblossom Highway' (1986), a brilliant photocollage of a landscape scene that could hardly be more different than the gently rolling green hills of East Yorkshire.

California and East Yorkshire, Hollywood and Bridlington. Hockney certainly inhabits two very different worlds.

Whereas Hockney's use of searingly bright colours in his Californian landscapes seems to have been accepted without much opposition, his renditions of Yorkshire landscapes in similarly exuberant colours have drawn accusations of gaudiness from some quarters. This is understandable, as Yorkshire does not enjoy the continuous bright sunshine of southern California or the same saturated colour scenery. But I think that Hockney's use of a surprisingly vivid palette for his Yorkshire pictures is a valid approach, as it opens up new ways of seeing that familiar landscape.

Of course, anyone who goes to Yorkshire expecting to see bright purple roads as in 'North Yorkshire' (1997) or turquoise hillsides as in 'Three Trees near Thixendale, Winter' (2007) will be disappointed. But, as Hockney has often said, he is not aiming for a photographic reproduction of a landscape. He is engaging with memories and emotions. He is producing art, not documentaries.

Hockney is brilliant at painting roads. In his landscapes, roads have a life of their own rather than being just an incidental feature. In 'Garrowby Hill' (1998), the way the road snakes down the hill towards the plain below makes the road resemble a living creature rather than just a means of getting from one place to another.

He gets a similarly powerful effect from a road in the wonderful 'South View on Warter, 20 August 2005'. In this picture, Hockney conjures up the feeling of freedom normally associated with the vast open spaces of the American West. A country road flows like a two-tone river from bottom left through the centre of the composition, with only telegraph wires, roadside hedges, and open fields in view. As with almost all his landscapes, there are no human figures, which increases the sense of freedom and space.

One wall of the exhibition space is taken up with thirty-six watercolours presented together as a single grid titled 'Midsummer: East Yorkshire' (2004). These thirty-six pictures could have constituted a very worthwhile exhibition in themselves. They were designed to be displayed this way, all thirty-six closely packed together in a grid. But some of the individual pictures are outstanding and could benefit from being displayed separately.

In his oil paintings, Hockney really does capture the spirit of the East Yorkshire land. 'Untitled Harvest' (2005) and 'Path through Wheatfield, July' (2005) celebrate unspectacular yet beautiful simple rural scenes, whilst the superb 'Kilham to Langtoft, 25 July 2005' perfectly sets off the breezy green and yellow of the fields with a heavily grey cloudy sky, a common summer sight in that part of the world.

Some pictures owe a clear debt to van Gogh, one of Hockney's heroes, such as 'Woldgate Vista, 27 July 2005' with its clear echoes of van Gogh's Provence paintings.

Other highlights of this amazing exhibition include the vast six-canvas oil painting 'The Road to Thwing, July, 2006', an upliftingly vibrant representation of high summer in farmland near Bridlington on the East Yorkshire coast; 'Woldgate Woods, 21, 23 and 29 November, 2006', with its gloriously warm red tones and long thin tree trunk shadows, a beautiful evocation of late autumn and early winter; and 'Woldgate before Kilham' (2007), a gorgeous two-canvas oil painting in the 'Hawthorn Blossom' series.

The gallery rooms at Burlington House are big enough to absorb the crowds at the Hockney exhibition. There isn't any need to jostle or employ elbows to get good views of the pictures. Visiting the exhibition is an uplifting experience.

After spending the morning at Burlington House, it's time to head up to Baker Street with all its Sherlock Holmes paraphernalia for today's film, *Extremely Loud & Incredibly Close*, which is showing at Everyman Baker Street cinema.

The film's crappy title, tear-jerking premise, and middle of the road cast do not bode well. However, I like the aerial views and street scenes of New York that appear in the trailer. So I decide to give the film a chance.

Located on the corner of Baker Street and Paddington Street, this Everyman cinema has a cosy atmosphere, comfortable seats and plenty of leg room. There is also a good bar downstairs near the auditorium. Horrendous covers of Bob Dylan songs are playing as background music before the adverts and trailers begin. I don't know who the bands are, but they are massacring Dylan's great songs.

The film starts and for what seems about half an hour, maybe more, I am groaning to myself, regretting having come to see it. It is as I had feared: Tom Hanks playing the salt of the earth nice guy, Sandra Bullock the perfect wife, John Goodman the kindly doorman, and so on. It's all very bland, very middle of the road, and uninspiring. But then there comes a turning point, after which the film suddenly becomes quite riveting and genuinely moving.

The crucial scene which galvanizes the whole film is the one where the kid plays back the recorded messages to the mute renter, played by Max von Sydow. Suddenly the film rings true, whereas until then it has merely been a plodding melodrama.

From that scene on, the film really is something special. *Extremely Loud & Incredibly Close* is certainly not devoid of Hollywood schmaltz, but it gets better and better as it goes on.

Although it doesn't ram it down your throat, the film has a clear message that despite the horror of the 9/11 attack on the city, the citizens of New York – or any other city – should not live their lives in fear. It is a useful warning against the unsavoury motives of reactionary figures in democracies who seek to exploit people's fear by constantly conjuring up the spectre of terrorist bogeymen. The film's unshakeable belief in the basic goodness of most people may be considered naïve by some, but I think it's a good standpoint.

Pleasantly surprised by how good *Extremely Loud & Incredibly Close* turns out to be, we come out the cinema and look around for somewhere to eat. Not far from the cinema, in an old-style arcade off Baker Street, we spot Nambu-Tei, a fairly downbeat but authentic-looking Japanese restaurant. We wash down the meal of sushi and fried chicken with some saké. It's an enjoyable meal, nothing special but not bad at all.

The Descendants

Coronet Notting Hill

Tate Britain down by the Thames at Millbank is holding a 'Picasso & Modern British Art' exhibition. I head along to it, not knowing quite what to expect. Will the exhibition be filled with paintings that make you go "What the hell is that?" or will it be more accessible to the interested non-expert? The last time I went to a modern art gallery it was a dismal experience, an exhibition full of dark twisted paintings that might have been therapeutic for the troubled artist but which offered little to the viewer.

But as soon as I get in to the 'Picasso & Modern British Art' exhibition my fears prove groundless. The exhibition is absolutely superb.

The main thrust of the exhibition is to demonstrate the often under-appreciated influence that Pablo Picasso had on modern British art.

Seven British artists are included in the exhibition, each of whom was influenced to varying degrees by Picasso. The featured British artists are Duncan Grant, Wyndham Lewis, Ben Nicholson, Henry Moore, Francis Bacon, Graham Sutherland and David Hockney.

Amongst the sixty Picassos on display, the ones that stand out for me are the beautiful cubist 'Jars and Lemon' (1907), purchased from Clovis Sagot's Galerie du Vingtième Siècle in Paris in October 1911 for the princely sum of £4; the intense and powerful 'Nude with Drapery' (1907); the impressionistic 'Blue Roofs, Paris' (1901), a lovely fresh and billowing city roof-top scene utterly different from Picasso's later cubist style; the simple but profound 'The Enamel Saucepan' (1945); 'Still Life with Garlands' (1918) with its unusual decorative frame; the cluttered yet exuberant 'Women of Algiers' (1955); and his magnificent 'The Three Dancers' (1925).

Highlights from the British contingent include Duncan Grant's sumptuous 'The Modelling Stand' (c.1914), his entrancing 'Interior at Gordon Square' (1914-15), and the part-abstract, part-figurative 'The White Jug' (1914-18). From Wyndham Lewis, the most outstanding exhibit is his wonderful 'Workshop' (c.1914-15), which looks better and better the further away you stand from it, so that its jumble of complex interlocking panes reveal their full force and energy to the eye.

Also excellent are Ben Nicholson's oddly touching '1933 (musical instruments' (1932-3); Henry Moore's amusingly unselfconscious 'Woman with Upraised Arms' (1924-5) and his brilliantly horrifying 'Three Points' bronze (1939-40); Francis Bacon's 'Interior of a Room' (1933-5), with its deep luxurious greens and purples; Graham Sutherland's perfectly balanced, warmly toned yet slightly disturbing 'Gorse on Sea Wall' (1939); and David Hockney's Polaroid joiner 'Still-Life Blue Guitar' (1982).

The exhibition is so good that I double back and do a second circuit to see everything twice before I leave the gallery. It's an exhibition that jolts you out of your normal way of seeing things. A great way to start the day.

Outside it's a fresh and sunny winter day, perfect for a leisurely wander along Millbank, past Lambeth Bridge and on up to the Houses of Parliament, culminating in a pit stop at St Stephen's Tavern on Bridge Street, Westminster.

St Stephen's is a pub with marvellous Victorian fittings and an elegant exterior with arched windows, sculpted columns and small head carvings sitting atop the pillars between each window. Inside, there is a beautiful curved wooden bar counter and a wonderful red coffered ceiling.

In St Stephen's I sink a pint of Tanglefoot ale, the winner of Bronze medals three years in a row at England's Taste of the West awards. Then I head on to the Salisbury pub a few minutes walk away in Covent Garden for another couple of drinks – a pint of Wells Bombardier, a reddish brown English Bitter that slides down very smoothly; and a pint of Timothy Taylor Landlord, a Yorkshire pale ale with a great flavour and soft feel.

The Salisbury is another Victorian tavern full of character. Various doorways lead into this pub from the adjoining streets. There is a large and welcoming island bar counter, staffed today by a friendly barman who is serving the customers efficiently but not impersonally. With the various doorways open, fresh air and sunlight are flowing into the bar and giving it a summery feel even though this is a February day.

Refreshed by the beers and the breezy atmosphere in the Salisbury, I go looking for somewhere for lunch. I strike lucky with Jamie's Italian on Upper St Martin's Lane. This restaurant is one of celebrity chef Jamie Oliver's burgeoning chain of Italian restaurants. They have done a great job in creating a restaurant that embodies Jamie Oliver's personality and outlook on life. There is a happy bustling atmosphere in the place, the waiter is enthusiastic and helpful without being pushy at all, and the food is great. The clientele is a diverse mix of tourists and local office workers, everyone enjoying the good food and the vibrant ambiance.

After the meal at Jamie's Italian I catch the Central Line underground train to Notting Hill Gate, the nearest station to the Coronet cinema where today's film *The Descendants* is showing.

The Coronet is a two-screen cinema. Originally built as a Victorian theatre in 1898, it is a beautiful building. Its grandeur is somewhat faded, but in a very appealing and characterful way. I like the circular entrance area; it immediately creates a sense of occasion as you enter the cinema.

I am slightly disappointed to see that *The Descendants* is showing in Screen 2, which is a nice enough auditorium but nothing remarkable, rather than the more splendid Screen 1 in which Hugh Grant and Julia Roberts appeared in one scene of *Notting Hill* and where British Prime Minister David Cameron watched the premiere of *Brokeback Mountain.* But Screen 2 is ok and you can sit wherever you like, rather than being corralled into a specific seat.

My expectations for *The Descendants* are pretty low. George Clooney is always great, but the trailer looks uninspiring. I have the feeling that we the audience are going to be asked to sympathize with a bratty daughter in a schmaltzy story.

However, the film turns out to be much better than I had feared. Not just Clooney but all the cast are very good. Though there is of course a sentimental dimension to the film, it is not syrupy and there are some very funny dialogue lines to balance the tragedy at the heart of the story.

The Hawaiian setting may have been de-glamourized as much as possible by the film makers, but it still looks beautiful. Yet what really gives the film its unique aura is the absolutely wonderful Hawaiian music soundtrack. It features stars of the genre such as Gabby Pahinui, Ray Kane, Keola Beamer, and Sonny Chillingworth. The music is gorgeous, creating a warm acoustic feel that perfectly complements the on-screen action.

Laura

BFI Southbank

Russell Square Gardens are looking very good this fine February morning. But in the café in a corner of the gardens, the decibel level is getting too high; a cacophonous combination of chairs scraping on the hard tiled floor and people speaking too loud. Outside is laidback and relaxed; inside is a persistent din.

It reminds me of a book I read a few years ago by Julian Treasure, titled Sound Business. That book is about the ways in which companies use – or more often neglect to use – sound in every part of their business. The book comes accompanied by a cd featuring some examples of good and bad use of sound. One such example is a short recording of a retail café, which demonstrates the difference in sound before and after the café's ceiling has been treated. The improvement is striking. Much more of the ambient sound is absorbed after the ceiling has been treated, leading to a more pleasant and relaxing environment.

But I don't know if just treating the ceiling would make much difference to the noise in this Russell Square Gardens café, as you are always going to get a racket when there is a hard floor with chairs getting scraped across it.

It's a relief to get out of the noisy café for the short walk to the British Museum. I have often walked past this museum without ever going in. With its Greek Revival style columns, the exterior of the building is very impressive. But the Norman Foster-designed Great Court interior is even more stunning. It's a great feeling to be standing at the same height as the top of some columns, which you can experience by ascending the curving staircases around the Reading Room in the centre of the Great Court. It's also good to get an elevated view of the amazing Haida totem pole, carved from a single cedar trunk, that towers up in one corner of the Great Court.

As lunch is beckoning I don't bother with the Grayson Perry exhibition, opting instead for a brief wander through the Enlightenment Gallery Room 1. Just the room itself is worth viewing, such is its magnificence. But the contents are fascinating too, arranged in seven sections: The Natural World, The Birth of Archaeology, Art and Civilisation, Classifying the World, Ancient Scripts, Religion and Ritual, and Trade and Discovery.

Amongst a multitude of wonders in this room, what particularly catches my eye is an orerry, a mechanical model of the solar system. It is mind-blowing to consider the immensity of the solar system represented in such a model. I gawp at this orerry for a while until pangs of hunger interrupt my reverie.

It's time for a mid-afternoon lunch feast at Maison Touareg on Greek Street.

Some great Arabic music is playing during the meal at Touareg. The harira soup and lentil soup are both delicious, as is the chicken couscous and the five mezze feast. The waitress is cheery and attentive. She shows great patience when it takes her several attempts to get our table to stop wobbling. Eventually she manages to wedge something under the table and it stabilizes the table enough to make it usable.

Very well fed, I exit Touareg and walk through the busy Friday afternoon streets to the Courtauld Gallery on the Strand. I had pre-ordered a ticket for the 'Mondrian and Nicholson' exhibition that is showing here today. That ticket was for the 10 a.m. entry slot. But these last couple of days some kind of bug has laid me low and drained me of energy, and I physically cannot get up early enough this morning to make that time slot. Better late than never, though, and I'm very glad I have made the effort to visit this gallery before closing time.

The 'Mondrian and Nicholson' exhibition is small scale but intriguing. It is hosted in just a couple of rooms up on the second floor. The exhibition traces the friendship and artistic relationship between Mondrian and Nicholson, focusing on the period during the 1930s when the two artists worked in neighbouring studios in Hampstead. At that time they were both leading figures in abstract art and their presence in London contributed to the artistic buzz in the city.

By the 1930s, Mondrian had dropped the second 'a' in his name. Until he was in his thirties, the Dutch painter's name was spelt Mondriaan, with double 'a'. Apparently, he decided to drop the second 'a' from his name in order to reduce the perception of him being a Dutch painter in favour of a more cosmopolitan, could-be-from-anywhere feel. This may have been partly due to a desire to distance himself from traditional Dutch associations with landscapes and the grey-brown palette of The Hague school artists.

It must have caused a bit of a kerfuffle back in his homeland when he so deliberately downplayed his origins. On the other hand, aesthetically you have to admire the economy and elegance of transforming your perceived origins through the deletion of a single letter in your name.

The Mondrian paintings on show in this exhibition are striking examples of his geometric abstraction period. They consist of strong white backgrounds overlaid with grids of vertical and horizontal black lines, with occasional patches of intense bright primary colours. It is all very abstract, nothing figurative at all, reflecting Mondrian's desire to create a new aesthetic of beauty and spirituality.

Mondrian said that his paintings aim for a dynamic equilibrium, a balance that reflects life itself. When you view paintings of his such as 'Composition with Yellow and Blue' (1932) or 'Composition B/(No II), with Red' (1935), you can feel this combination of dynamism and balance that Mondrian aspired to. The black lines of varying thickness pulse up and down and across the page, counterbalanced by small but stunningly vibrant bursts of primary colour placed at the edges of the compositions. In the same way that silence is something in itself and not just the absence of sound, the white in Mondrian's compositions has a vigour and life of its own rather than merely being a blank surface.

Mondrian is probably a tad austere for many people's taste, and he certainly didn't seem to make much effort to coin catchy titles for the works on show in this exhibition: 'Composition C (No.III), with Red, Yellow and Blue' (1935), for example, is not a particularly inspiring title. Yet that painting is the crowd-pleaser of this exhibition. The primary colours feature in far larger panes in this composition than in the others. By Mondrian's standards, this composition is almost gaudy. It is a great picture; it exemplifies his mastery of lines that intersect without ever looking like clichéd religious crosses, and his ability to achieve something beautiful and warm whilst remaining utterly abstract.

Ben Nicholson's paintings in this exhibition are equally abstract as those by Mondrian, but with a quite different feel. Nicholson uses a wider range of colour and shapes, and he also tends to construct his paintings from a vivid pane of colour somewhere fairly central in the composition from which the rest of the painting is layered outwards. It looks and feels very different from Mondrian's grids with splashes of colour usually pushed so far to the edge of the compositions that they seem to be barely hanging on.

One thing Nicholson and Mondrian shared, at this period anyway, was a predilection for abrupt unimaginative titles. Nicholson, for example, probably didn't exercise his imaginative faculties too much when he came up with the title '1937 (painting)'. Notwithstanding the uninspired titles, I like Nicholson's abstract paintings such as '1936 (painting)' and '1938 (painting – version I)'. These pictures' central burst of colour draws you in and then the surrounding planes play with your perception.

The 'Mondrian and Nicholson' exhibition is a very good taster of abstract art from the 1930s. But with this being the Courtauld Gallery, more delights await in the form of the superb permanent collection. It really is stunning to walk through the rooms on the first and second floors.

Everywhere you look, there is a masterpiece.

The paintings are perfectly lit, which is not the case in every gallery you visit. Here at the Courtauld, each painting has its own individual lamp attached, shining down but not directly onto the painting. This thoughtful lighting does full justice to the collection on display.

Another time I will come back to the Courtauld and linger longer over the permanent collection, but I have a film to catch over the river at BFI Southbank so off I go. At the gallery shop on my way out I am almost, but not quite, tempted to buy a Mondrian tea towel. Who needs a geometric abstract tea towel anyway? Instead I head out into the early evening rush hour on the Strand.

Walking across Waterloo Bridge at dusk on a fine day, as I do now after leaving the Courtauld Gallery, is to see London at its most beautiful. The wide sweep of the Thames, the Houses of Parliament, Saint Paul's Cathedral, it's all quite magical.

I walk slowly over Waterloo Bridge and pause for a while halfway across the river to admire the view in both directions. Even though there is no shortage of traffic, it feels far more serene out here on the bridge with its wide open views than it does in the hemmed-in city streets away from the Thames.

Cosily tucked in under the arches of Waterloo Bridge, BFI Southbank is a brilliant use of urban space. When I get here, the South Bank Book Market is just winding down. A smattering of bibliophiles are poring over the antique and vintage books set out on the temporary stalls. It's a great early evening atmosphere here on the riverside, quiet and calm but with the promise of the night to come.

The film I have come to see here at BFI Southbank is *Laura*, a 1944 film noir directed by Otto Preminger and starring Gene Tierney, Dana Andrews, Clifton Webb and Vincent Price. It's a sell-out screening this evening. This film has a dedicated following of fans who consider it to be a classic of the genre.

I enjoy the film, but for me it falls a little short of classic status. It is expertly directed, well acted and peppered with snappy deadpan dialogue. But it somehow lacks the sparkle that would elevate it to classic status.

Laura is certainly worth seeing, though. Gene Tierney is captivating as the Laura of the film title; Dana Andrews is entertaining as the cynical and lugubrious detective assigned to her case; and Vincent Price gives an intriguingly ambivalent portrayal of his character, Shelby Carpenter. But the outstanding performance in this film is by Clifton Webb as Waldo Lydecker, a sharp-tongued newspaper critic whose barbed remarks drip with witty sarcasm.

During one scene near the climax of the film, where Waldo has sneaked back into Laura's house unknown to either Laura or the police, one person in tonight's BFI audience lets out a yelp of horror as Waldo opens the door to reveal himself. That involuntary yelp sets off a ripple of laughter amongst the rest of the audience. It's a funny communal moment, the kind of experience you only get from watching a film in a cinema with people around you rather than watching dvds on your own at home.

At the end of the film there is a smattering of applause from the appreciative audience, and a lot of very positive comments.

"That was very good."

"Great."

"Fantastic."

Although the film was good, if I ever come again to Screen 3 here at BFI Southbank, I will get a seat on the front row where there is more leg room than further back in the auditorium. During today's showing, the person sitting behind me kept involuntarily kneeing the back of my seat. I couldn't help doing the same to the person sitting in front of me. Hopefully Screens 1 and 2 provide a bit more leg room in case I make future visits to this excellent venue.

Zéro de Conduite
L'Atalante

Riverside Studios

A Jean Vigo double bill at Riverside Studios lures me to Hammersmith this Saturday afternoon. On my way here on the Hammersmith Line train, a couple get on at one stop with their young son. All three are wearing blue Chelsea football shirts. Thankfully they are the only football fans on the train. It's not much fun being trapped in a train amongst a horde of raucous fans, but that Chelsea-supporting family of three are perfectly harmless.

Hammersmith is a busy bustling part of London. Riverside Studios, though, are located in a pleasantly quiet backwater down by the Thames. From the 1950s through to the 1970s, Riverside Studios was used by the BBC for such well loved productions as *Hancock's Half Hour*, *Doctor Who*, and *Play School*. After the BBC moved out, the venue was used by Channel 4 for their opening night launch party in 1982 and then in the 1990s it was the location for Chris Evans' *TFI Friday* programmes. The venue has got a lot of character and you can sense the television history that it has hosted.

Although there isn't time to indulge before the double bill starts, I have a quick peek in the bar restaurant area. I like the look of it, with its metallic church bell-like lamps hanging from the ceiling.

A stairway with attractive blue painted ironwork leads up to the cinema. The brick walls at either side of the auditorium are covered in tiled panels, which I assume were originally designed for soundproofing the room. There is a piano down by the screen, always a good sign; it shows that at least a modicum of taste influences the programming, and that occasionally an old silent film will be shown with live musical accompaniment.

With the uncomfortable experience of sitting in an auditorium with little leg room still fresh in my memory, I decide to do what I have not done for years and years: I go and sit in the front row.

A large pool of space separates the screen from the front row seats. It's a comfortable dark blue seat and I savour the limitless leg room. Because the screen is set well back from the front row, there isn't that abrupt, in-your-face looming of the screen that you would normally get when sitting in the front row of a cinema.

The first half of this afternoon's Jean Vigo double bill is his 1933 short film *Zéro de Conduite*, a forty-one minute recounting of the escapades and pranks of a bunch of rebellious adolescent boys at a repressive authoritarian boarding school in France. Despite its short running time, the film has a good rhythm and pacing.

Scenes of the boys' boisterous behaviour are interspersed with slower, more sedate scenes where the authority figures re-exert their control over the unruly boys.

There is not much character development in *Zéro de Conduite*, given the tight time constraints of this short film. Instead, the main thrust of the film seems to be its subversive, anti-authoritarian social comment. The viewer may not feel much empathy for the thinly sketched characters, but there is undeniable elegance in the film's critique of the social order of the day.

Quite a lengthy interval follows the end of *Zéro de Conduite*, presumably to fuel the takings at the bar, before the second half of the double bill gets underway with Jean Vigo's 1934 film *L'Atalante*.

This film is a masterpiece. Its visual impact is largely created by low camera shots looking up at the actors, which gives the characters an epic, heroic grandeur. This contrasts very effectively with the less than heroic, almost humdrum existence of the newly married lovebirds as they make their way on an industrial barge towards the bright lights of Paris.

The film also has documentary interest through its backdrop of 1930s industrialized France with its bustling docks, sprawling railway yards, and belching factories. It is not the type of setting you would normally associate with a romance, but it works.

Jean Dasté and Dita Parlo are perfect as the newly-weds whose marital bliss is short-lived under the pressure faced by the husband to get the barge to its destination in time to satisfy the company he is working for. But the most memorable performance in the film comes from the superb Michel Simon, whose coarse manner and bawdy antics as rough boozing sailor Le père Jules ensure that this film never lapses into the potential pitfalls of tear-jerking melodrama or kitchen-sink tedium.

Whereas the first half of today's double bill, *Zéro de Conduite*, is too short to be fully satisfying, the second half, the full length film *L'Atalante*, is superb. Feeling well entertained, after the double bill ends I exit the venue and nip through to the river by the narrow path that runs along the side of the Riverside Studios. Here on the banks of the Thames there is a beautiful view of the fast-flowing river, a crescent moon high in the pale blue sky, pink sunset clouds, and Hammersmith Bridge looking handsome in the early evening sunset.

I retrace my steps back past the Riverside Studios and take a quick look at the nearby Chancellors pub, with its "Come on Fulham" sign in the window, and then catch the Hammersmith Line train back into the city centre.

The day ends with a great meal at Bincho Japanese restaurant on Old Compton Street, Soho. Bincho has the swirling smoke and delicious smells that you want to find in a yakitori joint. Having spent three years in Tokyo and been spoiled by that city's incredible restaurant scene, I am delighted to find in Bincho a pretty good recreation of the vibrancy and atmosphere you get in such restaurants in Japan. We wolf down skewered chicken, fish, duck, rice, and salad, accompanied by Kirin and Sapporo beers. For a couple of hours, it's like being back in Tokyo.

The Best Exotic Marigold Hotel

Odeon Leicester Square

Screen 1 at Odeon Leicester Square is sensational: a huge screen and 1683 seats, the flagship cinema for the Odeon chain and the one where numerous film premieres are held. Tickets are expensive but worth it for the experience of seeing a film in such majestic surroundings.

But I won't sit in the Rear Stalls again, where I am for today's film, because from my seat in Row V the overhang is so long from the Circle above that I almost have to slide down in my seat to see the whole of the screen. Next time I'll go the whole hog and splash out on a ticket for a Circle seat.

Some of the other people in the cinema today must have been here before, as they knew to bring along little pocket torches to find their way to their seats. Without such a torch it is tricky to find your seat in this dark auditorium. But everyone eventually finds their seats.

Today's film, *The Best Exotic Marigold Hotel*, is absolutely wonderful. This is possibly the best feelgood movie I have ever seen. Visually, it is beautiful. The soundtrack features some brilliant music. And the acting, by an extraordinarily good, veteran cast, is perfect throughout.

The characters play off each other with a well sustained blend of ease and tension: Bill Nighy as the shy, geeky Douglas; Maggie Smith as the hardened-by-life Muriel, her xenophobia challenged by her encounters in India; Judi Dench as the determined yet vulnerable Evelyn; Tom Wilkinson suave as ever as the troubled Graham; Penelope Wilton as the uptight, narrow-minded Jean, unable to see the beauty and wonder around her in an unfamiliar environment; and Ronald Pickup very funny as the rakish Norman. Dev Patel and Tena Desae inject youthful energy into proceedings.

From the very first scene, I know that this is going to be a great film. The witty evocation of England's dreariness sets things up expertly and concisely for the India-based action. Some killjoy critics have panned the film, accusing it of showing an idealized India, but what did those idiots expect? If you want to see a gritty documentary about India, go see a gritty documentary, don't go to a feelgood romantic comedy.

The warm glow from *The Best Exotic Marigold Hotel* stays with me for hours after the film finishes.

7 Days in Havana

Odeon Covent Garden

The day's libations commence with a pint of Whitstable Bay Premium Ale at the Bloomsbury Tavern on Shaftesbury Avenue. The ale is smooth and has a very nice aftertaste. The Bloomsbury has great windows that feature stained glass heraldic images, a fine sight to take in while quaffing the beer. The stained glass above the beautiful curved doorway is particularly stunning, a flourish of curvaceous extravagance for what is actually a very down-to-earth boozer once you get inside.

After the ale aperitif we make the short walk along to Jamie's Italian restaurant in Covent Garden for lunch. The starters of chestnut mushrooms and pasta are very good. The mains of whole bream are bony but delicious. For dessert we have almond tart and the best tiramisu I've ever had. The meal is washed down with four glasses of white wine: a Pinot Grigio that is ok but nothing special; two glasses of the excellent Verdicchio; and one glass of Fiano.

It's a great meal in a bustling yet relaxed atmosphere.

Well fed and mellow after the nice long lunch, we stroll to Odeon Covent Garden where today's film beckons. The exterior of Odeon Covent Garden is very eyecatching with its 129-foot long bas-relief frieze by sculptor Gilbert Bayes. The theme of the frieze is 'Drama Through the Ages', reflecting the building's original use as a theatre when it opened in 1931.

Unfortunately most of the building's art deco splendour was lost when the interior was gutted in 1970 during the conversion of the venue from a theatre into a cinema. Screen 4 where today's film is showing has a fair-sized screen, but the auditorium is short on atmosphere.

The film on show is *7 Days in Havana*. It turns out to be very good, much better than one would think from the lukewarm-to-hostile reviews it seems to have received. The film comprises a series of seven shorts, each directed by a different director, covering consecutive days of a week in Havana. The directors are Laurent Cantet, Benicio Del Toro, Julio Medem, Elia Suleiman, Juan Carlos Tabio, Pablo Trapero, and Gaspar Noé.

The 'Monday' film features a young American drama student in Havana, who picks up what he thinks is a Cuban woman but who turns out to be a man. The curiosity, goodwill and naivety of the young American are engagingly portrayed. Because a lot of viewers will already have seen *The Crying Game*, the revelation that she is a he doesn't carry the shock factor that it otherwise would do. Yet the 'Monday' section is a well told story and goes beyond the usual Havana postcard clichés, regardless of many critics' claims to the contrary.

Onto the 'Tuesday' film, which is carried wonderfully by Emir Kusturica. A sozzled Kusturica constantly escapes his film-festival handlers, as he lurches around very entertainingly from one Havana location to another. There is a fantastic scene where the local taxi driver who is driving him around takes him to a jam session and starts to play the trumpet brilliantly. This is the best moment of the film: as the trumpeter plays, the camera lingers for a few seconds in close-up on the watching Kusturica's face. Although Kusturica doesn't say anything at that point, you can read on his face his appreciation of the trumpeter's brilliance. Kusturica in that simple moment gives a subtle and profound acknowledgement of the trumpeter's talent and charisma.

In the 'Wednesday' film, 'The Temptation of Cecilia', a Spanish music promoter on a talent-spotting visit to Havana offers Cecilia, a Cuban singer, the opportunity to go to Spain to perform in clubs there. She is tempted, not only by that offer but also by the Spanish guy himself. Her baseball-playing partner drinks himself unconscious when he finds out he has been jilted. Without hammering home the point too crudely, this short film gives a touching vignette of the love-versus-money dilemma that life can put you in.

The 'Thursday' short is about journalist Elia Suleiman trying to get an interview with Fidel Castro, which doesn't happen because Fidel makes an interminable speech. In a very deadpan downbeat way, this section of the film is extremely funny. Suleiman perfectly embodies the strange experience of being utterly alone in a wonderful place.

There is a great scene in which Suleiman goes down to the seafront where he sees various locals, all of them apparently alone, motionless by the sea. They are either looking out to sea or just sitting by the sea, seemingly ignoring it. The contrast is very effective between the passive immobility of the people in the scene and the energy of the sea waves as they crash on the shore, and the wind blowing through a tree in the foreground.

The 'Friday' film focuses on the exorcism of a girl's lesbianism. This is an uncomfortable portion of the overall film. It is not pleasant to watch the girl being subjected to a ritualistic exorcism. This vaguely malevolent short certainly does not fall into any kind of postcard cliché of Havana.

In the 'Saturday' short, electricity cuts drive a woman crazy as she tries to prepare some pastries for that evening. This short portrays a tragi-comic version of life in Havana. It ends very sadly, with Cecilia leaving Cuba on a raft, leaving her parents distraught when they find out that she has left them and the island.

The Sunday film is dominated by Marta, a larger than life character cajoling her neighbours to pitch in to prepare a party for Ochun. This is a funny segment of the overall film, with a great scene at the party where the singing is led by a wonderfully charismatic guest. It is very nicely edited, going from the party to a shot of Marta sitting sleepily, alone, in her apartment after the party has finished and everyone has gone home.

I really enjoy *7 Days in Havana*. It doesn't bother me that the separate short films that it is comprised of don't really hang together; what do you expect from seven different directors and seven different stories? The stories are all engaging slices of life in a fabled city. I like the changes of tempo and feel from one story to the next, and the music is superb.

After the film, we head up Southampton Row via Woburn Place and Euston Road to take a look at the refurbished Kings Cross railway station. What a transformation from the sleazy dump it used to be! I am stunned. Who would have thought that you would be able to eat sushi in Kings Cross station. The swirling design in the new concourse gives an uplifting vibrant feel to the place, and the exterior yellow brick facade has been given a thorough scrub to restore it to its original splendour.

Marina Abramovic: The Artist is Present

Institute of Contemporary Arts

Greenwich is a part of London I have never visited before. So I'm happy to have a jaunt out here for lunch with a friend who lives in the area. From Holborn in central London, I take the Central Line east-bound underground train to Bank station. At Bank, I change onto the Docklands Light Railway to Cutty Sark. The DLR from Bank passes through some evocative maritime station names as it heads towards Greenwich: Canary Wharf, Heron Quays, Island Gardens, and so on. One of the stations is called Mudchute, not a particularly attractive place name.

There are annoying taped announcements on the DLR train out to Greenwich. It keeps repeating the first two or three words of each announcement and also sometimes the final two or three words: "This is. This is the train to Lewisham", or "Please take your bags with you. With you."

I get to Greenwich with about three-quarters of an hour to spare before my lunch appointment, so before that I have a wander along the bank of the River

Thames as far as the Trafalgar Tavern. The Trafalgar's faded grandeur is very appealing. By the tavern's entrance door, a mother is trying to take a picture of her teenage child, who is reluctant to be photographed. The kid is standing next to the statue of Lord Nelson. "Smile", commands the mother. "Smile. Open your mouth. Open your mouth. That's better." Click.

It's good to wander along the Thames in Greenwich and drink in the fresh air, the breezy almost windswept openness which you don't get in central London.

Having met up with my friend, we have lunch in the beer garden of well known Greenwich pub The Gipsy Moth, which is located just a few yards away from the recently restored Cutty Sark. The Cutty Sark ship is much bigger than I expected it to be. It looks superb. I can imagine what an incredibly fine sight the Cutty Sark must have been in full sail out on the ocean.

In the Gipsy Moth beer garden we have a delicious lunch of breaded chicken, washed down with a couple of pints of guest ales.

It was great to venture out to Greenwich, but today's film draws me back to central London. Lunch had been quite early so there is time for a pre-film meal at Toku restaurant in Regent Street. This restaurant describes its style as contemporary Japanese cuisine. The chicken and rice is good. The nigiri sushi assortment is ok but unfortunately comes with dabs of wasabi, which I don't like. It has been so long since I have eaten in a Japanese restaurant that I forget to specify that I want the sushi without wasabi.

I have a bottle of Kirin beer to accompany the food. We would have had cake but after half an hour of waiting, no waiter comes to take our order so we get up and leave and get a cappucino and cake at the nearby Pret A Manger instead.

From Regent Street, I walk down Waterloo Place towards The Mall. The film I am going to see is *Marina Abramović: The Artist is Present*, at the Institute of Contemporary Arts.

Tonight's showing is almost sold out. The audience is arty, as you would expect for such a film and in this venue, but good humoured and affable too. It isn't a pretentious vibe at all. Everyone is here to enjoy the film and the evening. Relaxed happy chatter fills the auditorium before the film starts, and there is an equally happy vibe after the film finishes.

Screen 2 at ICA is very good, a cosy auditorium with comfy red seats. Tasteful, laidback jazz is playing before the film starts.

"Proscenium or not?" asks one member of the audience to the friend he is sitting next to in the row in front of me.

They have been talking about a theatre. It's not a question I have ever heard before, and judging from the silence with which the question is met, the questioner's friend isn't too sure what a proscenium is.

"The bit of the stage in front of the curtain", the guy helpfully elaborates.

I have come to tonight's film with an open mind, though I can't help harbouring a modicum of scepticism. Will it be a pile of pretentious crap or something really interesting?

The prospect of watching a two-hour documentary about a Serbian performance artist has me intrigued, although wary. If it puts me to sleep, will I embarrass myself by snoring out loud? Will there be anyone else there to watch it anyway? What is the big deal about a performance artist spending three months in New York's Museum of Modern Art sitting on a chair staring at somebody sitting opposite her?

But my initial scepticism evaporates as soon as the film gets under way. The film is superb.

The key theme of the film is that silence, slowness, and emptiness are under-appreciated in today's society. Through her performance art, particularly the performance where visitors sit opposite the artist and the two individuals simply look at each other in silence for up to fifteen minutes, Marina Abramović wants to create a space in which she and the audience member reach a kind of communion of slow silence.

It is very moving. Many visitors sitting opposite Abramović have tears streaming down their faces.

Ulay, the German performance artist with whom Abramović had an intense relationship for over a decade, appears in this documentary as being equally charismatic as Abramović but not possessed by the same drive and ambition. The film shows how they terminate their relationship in epic style. Starting from different ends, they each walk the Great Wall of China, meet in the middle, and say goodbye to each other. Ulay starts his journey from the Gobi Desert. Abramović starts her journey from the Yellow Sea. As bold dramatic gestures go, you cannot beat this for a relationship breakup.

The film also provides fascinating glimpses of the preparation for the MOMA show, the curator, the security staff, the visitors to the show, and the young performance artists recreating Abramović's earlier performances. Well paced, good atmospheric music runs through this captivating film.

I emerge from the cinema at about half past nine in the evening. The July sky is a beautiful light blue. The ICA cinema nestles harmoniously within elegant and imposing Nash House. I head up the nearby Duke of York Steps, enjoying this blissful summer evening in London.

Woody Allen: A Documentary

Odeon Panton Street

Lunch today is at a tapas restaurant in Soho. The food is reasonably good. We have scallops, apple and fennel salad, and albondigas tapas. These are ok but nothing special. The chicken couscous is good. But I won't go back to this restaurant because of the extraordinarily sloppy service.

The waitresses ask if we want to see the dessert menu after we have finished our starters but before the main course has arrived; they take the bottle of wine away after pouring the first glasses but then do not bring the bottle back to refill our glasses when they are empty and need replenishing; they bring the main course but not any cutlery, saying that they will bring cutlery but then they don't; and they pour the last of the wine unevenly, pouring a tiny amount of wine into my companion's glass and twice as much into my glass so that my glass is almost overflowing whilst my companion's glass is almost empty.

Regretting the choice of restaurant, I head over to Panton Street Odeon, where *Woody Allen: A Documentary* is showing in Screen 2. The film turns out to be wonderful.

The film gives interesting insights into Woody Allen's early days as a gag writer, followed by his foray into stand-up comedy. As a performer, at first Allen is reluctant and nervous on stage. But then he suddenly finds his style at one triumphant gig where everything clicks for the first time. Unfortunately that particular night was not filmed so we don't get to see it, but it is described vividly by someone who was there.

It is also interesting to hear about how Woody Allen very early in his career gained almost unprecedented control over his films as director rather than just as writer. We see how his early films are for laughs, evolving as time goes by into more mature and story-driven films with fleshed-out characters. In this lovingly crafted documentary there is a good mix of comments and perspectives from industry people such as Martin Scorsese, Larry David, John Cusack, Scarlett Johansson and others, as well as interviews with the man himself and clips from his films.

Although there is nothing startlingly revelatory in this documentary, it is a joy to watch for fans of Woody Allen films. It's good to listen to him speaking as snow falls outside his Manhattan window during the interview.

After the film I walk through intermittent rain along Shaftesbury Avenue, then past the University of London Senate House building on Bedford Way. I pause for a few moments to look in awe at the building's stunningly imposing 1930s art deco architecture.

Anna Karenina

Phoenix Cinema

East Finchley tube station is a station worth lingering at for a few minutes, instead of bolting out of it the instant you have stepped off a train there. The station building is wonderful.

Standing on the platform is like stepping back in time to the 1930s.

Designed by Charles Holden, one of the country's leading architects of the period, one of the station's most striking features are the two semi-circular towers on opposite platforms, joined by a bridge over the railway track, like glass goalposts and a brick crossbar. According to the Royal Institute of British Architects, that design is an echo of Walter Gropius' model factory at the 1914 Werkbund Exhibition.

Another superb feature is the art deco statue of an archer by sculptor Eric Aumonier. The statue exudes a tremendous blend of poise and power. It has a boldness that you would associate with New York's art deco splendours in the streets of Manhattan rather than with this relatively quiet London suburb. But it fits the station and its environment perfectly.

What has drawn me to East Finchley is the chance to see a film at the Phoenix, one of London's best-loved cinemas. The Phoenix was built in 1910 as a single-screen cinema. It is just a few minutes walk north from the station along the High Road.

On the way I spot a tv celebrity – Huw Edwards, the BBC newsreader whose warm Welsh accent is so soothing and reassuring. He is walking along the High Road with a companion. Both their faces are taut and grim, as if they have had an argument and have not yet made up. But when I watch the evening news later that night, I realise that that severe facial expression is actually his normal one.

The Phoenix cinema has a sleek and uncluttered modernist exterior enlivened by the bold splash of orange colour provided by the phoenix plaque in the postage stamp corner of the building. Inside, there is a nicely jumbled up lobby and an upstairs café bar area with some interesting artwork on the wall at the top of the stairs. I am pleasantly surprised to see Scottish Deuchars IPA on the beer list. I order a pint and quaff it while waiting for the 5.30 p.m. screening of today's film, *Anna Karenina*.

The cinema auditorium is fabulous. Its 1910 barrel-vaulted ceiling, wonderful art deco wall panels from 1938, and the bronze and red colour scheme give the place a cosy opulence that is quite stunning. The curved backs of the seats give a pleasing sensation of waves at sea rippling from the back of the auditorium down towards the screen.

If you judge it only from the official trailer, you might assume that this version of *Anna Karenina*, directed by Joe Wright and adapted from Tolstoy by Sir Tom Stoppard, is little more than a pompous costume drama. But I'm glad I didn't let the trailer put me off, because the film turns out to be riveting.

The cast are clearly revelling in the period splendour, but there is plenty humour bubbling away under the surface. A playfulness in the acting provides a surprising but effective counterbalance to the heavy tragedy that steadily unfolds.

Previously I haven't been a huge fan of Keira Knightley, but in this film she is terrific. As Anna Karenina, she embodies dashing enthusiasm and fragile vulnerability in equal measure. Visually the film is gorgeous to look at, with its opulent sets and costumes, beautifully lit and filmed.

One of the most striking scenes in the film is the one in the theatre when time seems to stand still as the entire audience turn their judgemental eyes onto Anna. Without any superfluous dialogue or other signals to the audience, at that moment you know that Anna is doomed.

The Phoenix is the perfect cinema to watch this film in. The glorious auditorium mirrors the feel of the splendour unfolding on screen. Watching *Anna*

Karenina in this superb cinema has been a wonderful experience.

It's good to have seen the captivating 1930s design of East Finchley station in daylight when I arrived here earlier today, as well as seeing it after dark when I leave. Illuminated in the mid-evening darkness, the station looks even more like a magical 1930s alternate universe than it had done earlier in the afternoon daylight.

Lawless

Aubin Cinema

At Liverpool Street station I stop for a few moments to admire the handsome, white marble on red brick Great Eastern Railway memorial to those railway staff who died during the First World War. The memorial was unveiled in 1922 by Field Marshall Sir Henry Wilson, who was assassinated on his way home after the ceremony by two members of the Irish Republican Army.

When I emerge from Liverpool Street station it takes me a few seconds to get my bearings, not having been here before. I head along Bishopsgate. Just after Woodin's Shades pub, with its wonderful stained glass above the entrance doorway, I turn right towards Spitalfields Market. Inside the market at Canteen restaurant I have a very good lunch of sea bass with beetroot and fennel salad, washed down with a couple of pints of Meantime, a nice crisp India Pale Ale from the microbrewery at Greenwich.

Outside it's a bright breezy blue sky afternoon. I trundle over from Spitalfields Market to the shabby elegance of The Ten Bells pub on Commercial Street.

Here I quaff a pint of Truman's Runner, an East London bitter that is ok but nothing special. The main reason for coming here is to see the very impressive wall tiling that dates from around 1900. It's very well preserved and adds a lot of character to the place. The graffiti in the toilets is a bit disturbing, though.

Out again into the afternoon sun, and I make my way generally in the direction of the Aubin cinema for today's film, *Lawless*. On the way there, from Shoreditch High Street I spot the surreal sight of two abandoned Underground trains perched above what looks like a derelict night club, the two trains looking like they could start moving at any time and come crashing down onto the street below. It's an almost apocalyptic scene.

Redchurch Street, where the Aubin cinema is located, has an edgy radical vibe quite different from other parts of London. The cinema is housed in the basement of a two-storey yellow-brick building. The auditorium is a cosy compact fifty-seater with luxurious velvet chairs to sink into.

Johnny Cash's 'Get Rhythm' is playing as I enter the auditorium, which gets this place an immediate thumbs up from me. Other Johnny Cash classics follow, including 'Ring of Fire', 'Don't Take Your Guns To Town', and 'Five Feet High and Rising'. This is perfect music to have playing before tonight's film, *Lawless*.

My seat is A5 on the front row, very close to the screen. There is a nice intimate atmosphere in this cinema. The film I have come here to see, *Lawless*, is directed by John Hillcoat and stars Shia LeBeouf, Tom Hardy, Guy Pearce, Jessica Chastain, Mia Wasikowska, and Gary Oldman. It is a very good cast. But what makes this film for me is the great soundtrack: rough, sawing country fiddle and the sublime Emmylou Harris at regular intervals, capped with Willie Nelson singing 'Midnight Run' over the closing credits. Bliss! Nick Cave wrote the screenplay for *Lawless* and his impeccable taste in music strongly influences the superb soundtrack to the film.

Set in early 1930s, Prohibition-era rural Virginia, *Lawless* is based on the biographical novel by Matt Bondurant, grandson of one of the main characters that appear in the film. It's a very violent film, but brilliantly made and gripping to watch.

Shia LeBeouf, Tom Hardy and Jason Clarke are very good as brothers Jack, Forrest and Howard Bondurant respectively, bootleggers who get dragged into an increasingly brutal fight with the law. Jack is the kid brother whose entrepreneurial drive lands him in hot water; Forrest is the taciturn and grunting rock upon which the Bondurant bootlegging operation is built; and Howard is the wildest and most dishevelled of the brothers. They find themselves up against the law in the shape of Guy Pearce's special agent Charlie Rakes, a sadistic fop drafted in from Chicago to put these bootlegging country boys in their place.

Without having been there it's not possible for me to vouch for the authenticity of the 1930s rural Virginia setting, but the film feels very evocative of that time and place. The characters are all well played and believable, and the story is well paced and pulsating.

"It was sooooo violent!" says one member of the audience to her friend outside the cinema as everyone is leaving.

Her friend replies, "It was majorly violent. I really liked it though."

The Eye of the Storm

Clapham Picturehouse

Cittie of Yorke pub, as its name suggests, is an 'olde Englishe' style place. It has the most incredible interior. From the street it looks very good, with an elegant and refined facade. But it's the inside that takes your breath away. When you enter the main room it's like stepping back several centuries in time. It feels almost like a church, but devoted to alcohol.

Huge wine vats sit on sturdy shelves above the bar. Stained glass windows loom high up at the far end of the hall, and several very inviting intimate booths offer a degree of privacy if that is what you are after. It's an amazingly atmospheric pub.

I order a pint of Sam Smith's Organic Lager. It's clean and fresh but short on flavour. As I'm drinking it, I suddenly hear a loud jangling noise. For a moment or two I wonder what is making the noise. Then all is revealed. A group of Morris dancers enter the pub in full regalia. It is the bells on their clogs that is making the jangling sound. The traditionally attired dancers' presence in this historical setting reinforces the odd feeling of having stepped back centuries in time.

From the Citttie of Yorke I head on to another landmark London pub, the art nouveau and arts and crafts styled Blackfriar. Approached from Blackfriars Bridge, the narrow wedge-shaped Blackfriar pub building resembles a much smaller version of New York's Flatiron Building.

Inside, Blackfriar is as stunning as the Cittie of Yorke but in a completely different way, with a more extravagant decorative style featuring sculptures, reliefs, and a beautiful mosaic tiled ceiling in the far back room. It is an incredible interior. I am happy to linger here for a while, taking in the surroundings while I sink a pint of Pure Gold ale followed by one of Suffolk Blonde. What a great pub.

Today's film, *The Eye of the Storm*, is showing at the Clapham Picturehouse. So I take the Northern Line train to Clapham Common and walk the short distance from that station to the cinema on Venn Street.

A few minutes further on from the cinema I come across a beautiful old Post Office doorway with 'Postmens Office' written above it in elegant tall script. An adjacent date plaque has the year 1902 carved into it in wonderfully curved numbering that could be either art nouveau or arts and crafts. Whichever style it is, it looks superb.

I didn't know it when I booked my ticket, but the showing here at the Clapham Picturehouse tonight is the UK premiere of *The Eye of the Storm*. It is part of Film Fest Australia, which is being held this weekend at the Clapham Picturehouse and then next weekend at the Hackney Picturehouse.

It's a sold-out showing. When all the audience are in their seats, someone introduces the film from the stage and gives profuse thanks to the Australian High Commission for their support in making it possible to show the film. The film is directed by Fred Schepisi, with a screenplay by Judy Morris based on the novel by Patrick White. Geoffrey Rush, Charlotte Rampling and Judy Davis are the stars.

Before the film begins there is a tangible sense of excited anticipation in the auditorium. But as the film proceeds, you can almost taste the disappointment in the air. The eager pre-film buzz mutates into a sullen silence amongst the audience, as it becomes painfully clear that the film stinks. It's a turgid melodrama peopled by such selfish, privileged yet self-pitying characters that you just don't care what happens to any of them. It is all very lovey-dovey and self-indulgent.

During most of the second half of the film there is some very loud stomach-rumbling from the bloke sitting in front of me, which provides some welcome light relief from this mildly depressing film.

Not a single person applauds at the end of *The Eye of the Storm*, despite this being the UK premiere with a cheerful atmosphere pre-film. When the film ends and puts us out of our misery, the audience appears to have temporarily lost the will to live.

It's a subdued and dispirited audience that shuffles dejectedly out the auditorium.

Double Indemnity

The Lexi Cinema

Chicken couscous and a couple of glasses of white wine at Touareg restaurant on Greek Street; it's a very good lunch, with unexpected entertainment provided in the form of a transvestite run that passes by the window half-way through the meal. The runners come from Soho direction and their attire is eyecatching: bright pink and yellow costumes, with many runners tottering past on high heels, not the most efficient footwear for a run but very entertaining for onlookers. One runner has even brought along his dog on a lead.

Everyone in the restaurant has stopped eating and is grinning through the windows at this bizarre spectacle.

After lunch I take the Bakerloo Line from Oxford Circus to Queen's Park and walk from there to Chamberlayne Road in Kensal Rise, where today's destination cinema, The Lexi, is showing the 1944 film noir classic *Double Indemnity*. I have some time to kill before the film starts, so I go for a leisurely wander round the streets in the vicinity of the cinema. Kensal

Rise is a nice residential area, quietly prosperous in an unshowy but contented way.

As I pass a house on Purves Road, a woman says, "What are you doing outside, naughty girl? Back garden please", as she scoops up her cat and carries it through the house to the back garden.

Back at the Lexi, the box office person tells me, "You'll need to wait here for a few minutes till it's been cleaned up inside. There's a mountain of popcorn from a kids' party."

The Lexi is a social enterprise rather than a commercial cinema and all profits go to the Sustainability Institute. It has a good, community feel, much more personal and friendly than mainstream cinemas. The auditorium has a homely feel. Down at the front near the screen there are two small round wooden tables each with a candle on it. The first two rows of seating consist of freestanding armchairs. Behind them are a few rows of fixed seats with cupholders into which I slide the beer I have bought from the tiny bar at the back of the building.

Hanging from the auditorium ceiling are a strange shoal of light bulbs which occasionally change colour. Apart from me, the only other person sitting in the darkened auditorium before the film starts is one spectator who is on a seat near the back of the room. The projectionist doesn't notice her and gets a shock when she is testing the screen for sharpness of focus and the unseen spectator suddenly barks out, "Are you going to show this for me?"

The projectionist and I can't help laughing at this unexpected, brusque question from the dark depths of the room.

When the film starts there is only me and that one other person in the audience. But two minutes into the film, a third person appears and sits down right in front of me, partially blocking my view of the screen, even though he could have sat anywhere else in the room. What kind of inconsiderate person sits in front of one of only two people in an otherwise empty auditorium? So I move a few seats over and enjoy the rest of the film without the back of that bloke's head part blocking my view.

What a great film *Double Indemnity* is. It is an absolute masterpiece, not just of film noir but of any genre. Based on the novel by James M. Cain, the screenplay is written by Billy Wilder and Raymond Chandler. The hardboiled Chandleresque dialogue is utterly superb. Any fan of Chandler's novels will love this.

Sitting here in the Lexi watching the film, I feel like applauding the brilliantly cynical and witty lines perfectly delivered by stars Fred MacMurray and Barbara Stanwyck.

Stanwyck plays Phyllis Dietrichson, a seductive femme fatale who lures MacMurray's character, Walter Neff, into a plot to murder her husband. You can see why Barbara Stanwyck was the biggest female star in Hollywood in that era. She is cool, sexy, sharp and tough. MacMurray's character is no match for her. Walter Neff is a slick insurance salesman who realizes that he is getting out of his depth by agreeing to assist Phyllis in murdering her husband in order to cash in on his fifty-thousand dollar accident insurance policy.

Even though Walter is complicit in the murder, the way MacMurray plays the character makes you sympathize with him through to the end. Walter is not a one-dimensional evil villain. Far from it; he is a good-natured everyday kind of person who reacts in a plausible way to the seductive opportunity that is presented to him. A streak of detached arrogance in Walter also ensures that he is not just a naïve simpleton taken in by a scheming woman.

There is a moral ambivalence about the film that must have been quite radical back in the more puritanical era of film censorship that prevailed in the 1940s when *Double Indemnity* was first released.

Stanwyck and MacMurray are good enough to have carried this film on their own. But there is a wonderful added bonus in the role played by Edward G. Robinson as Barton Keyes, Walter's boss. Keyes is a claims manager at the company where Walter works. The deep affection that each feels for the other, despite the untrusting business of insurance claims that they work in, adds an emotional dimension to the film that you wouldn't get in inferior examples of film noir.

Robinson is a class act; he is hugely entertaining and impressive every second he is on screen.

A lot of credit for the artistic and commercial success of *Double Indemnity* has to go to director of photography John F. Seitz. The interior scenes are very dark, even for the film noir genre, and this intensifies the oppressive inevitability of the film's murderous denouement. The dark, emotionally charged interiors contrast effectively with the beautiful carefree California exteriors, typified in the Spanish Colonial house up in Hollywood Hills where Walter and Phyllis hatch their plot. From the outside, it is idyllic, the kind of place most people would love to live; inside, a banal evil drifts.

Sightseers

Prince Charles Cinema

The barmaid's attitude here in this Bloomsbury pub is less than welcoming. My innocuous question, "Are you serving food?", is met with barely a nod, accompanied by a look of disdain. She has a sullen look on her face. It's as if my query is such a drag, such an imposition.

She doesn't bother saying anything in reply to my question, so I press on regardless and read off what I want from the menu. I am too hungry to be discouraged by her indifference. The soup of the day is split pea soup and I order that plus lamb pie as the main course.

It's around two in the afternoon and quiet in here, only a couple of other tables occupied. I sit at a corner table and admire the pub's wonderful interior. The snob screens seem very small, so tiny that you wonder how they can offer any privacy at all.

The barmaid appears a few minutes later.

"If it's all right with sir, I bring the soup and the main course at the same time", she says, plonking the two courses down without waiting to hear from sir if this is ok.

For half a second I consider asking her to take the main course away and bring it when I have finished the soup, but I see the look on her face and decide against that. From her demeanour thus far, I shudder to think what she might do to my main course if I tell her to take it away and then bring it back when I am ready for it.

When some other customers enter the pub a few minutes later, she is quite friendly towards them. They seem to know each other. Maybe it is just with strangers that it's up with the barricades.

The soup is good and the lamb pie is delicious, with much better prepared vegetable accompaniments than you would normally get in a British pub. The drink is excellent too, a pint of St Austell Tribute, an ale with a beautiful golden colour.

As I'm eating, a couple come in. The guy tells the barmaid, "I've made a resolution not to drink for the rest of this month", which begs the question, what is he doing in a bar?

The other person working behind the bar is an older guy who is very friendly, the antithesis of the barmaid. He asks how my pie is, and he has a very kindly manner in his dealings with all the other customers who are in here at the moment. Hopefully his hospitable example will rub off on his less welcoming colleague. If I had been served by him when I came in, I would have had a much better feeling than the one I was left with by the surly barmaid.

Princess Louise in Holborn is my next destination. It's bustling and lively at 3.15 p.m. this Thursday afternoon. Amazing decor in this bar. Great booths along each side of the polished wooden bar counter. I have a bottle of Taddy Porter, dark, big flavour, not too treacly. There's a beautiful clock in the carved wooden arch in the middle of the bar.

The Prince Charles Cinema, tucked up a side street off Leicester Square, is my cinema of choice today. Famous in London for its exuberant singalong showings of films such as *Grease*, *The Sound of Music*, and *The Rocky Horror Picture Show*, the Prince Charles is also currently showing a 'quote along' showing of 2004 zombie romcom *Shaun of the Dead*.

The film that I have come to see today, the British psycho-comedy road trip *Sightseers*, fits nicely into the Prince Charles' off-the-wall programming ethos. This early evening showing takes place in the upstairs auditorium, a compact atmospheric space under a low ceiling with little pinpricks of light showing through like stars in a dark sky.

The low ceiling adds to the cosy intimate vibe.

It's a sold-out showing and tonight's audience is already in high spirits even before the trailers start. I have a feeling *Sightseers* is going to go down well with this boisterous crowd.

After the opening scenes in which we see Tina (Alice Lowe) and Chris (Steve Oram) getting ready to set off on their holiday romance, *Sightseers* quickly and wonderfully turns into *Natural Born Killers* with an English Midlands accent.

Instead of the stereotypical paraphernalia of American road trip movies such as truckstops, honky tonks, and panoramic desert vistas, in *Sightseers* there are dull caravan parks, a ride on a preserved tram with commentary provided by a uniformed tour guide, and a visit to a pencil museum.

In their delicious cringeworthiness, the film's humdrum settings and tedious holiday activities evoke a spirit similar to the Alan Partridge tv series; the numbing banality of drab existence offset by doses of humour rooted in loneliness, awkwardness, and frustrated ambition.

Sightseers is certainly funny but it also conveys an air of existential desperation that leaves you uneasy even when you are laughing along with the funny bits.

The two stars of *Sightseers*, Alice Lowe and Steve Oram, also wrote the screenplay and as you watch the film unfold you sense that this is a labour of love brilliantly realized. Lowe and Oram play off each other wonderfully. She is fragile and vulnerable but with a feistiness that reaches perfect expression in the closing scene in which she and Oram are standing on top of a railway viaduct. He, on the other hand, plays the assertive male, consumed by his obsessions, sinking steadily and irrevocably into vindictive madness directed towards a society that he feels has rejected him and his world view.

His deranged contribution to keeping Britain tidy is stomach-churning; his jealousy of higher-achieving individuals than himself plunges him into a murderous rage; and his contempt for Daily Mail readers encapsulates this film's weirdly effective blend of humour and callousness.

The film contains some gore that not everyone will want to see. But with its precise characterization, brooding atmosphere and superb script, I think that *Sightseers* will enjoy a well deserved cult status in years to come.

It's fresh and breezy this evening after the film as I walk past Russell Square gardens in Bloomsbury. At the edge of the gardens, near the railings where I pass by, I can hear someone saying to the person he is with, "I'm doing this for you, I'm doing this for us. I'm making a move." There is an urgent, almost pleading tone in his voice. I walk on and don't hear how that anguished conversation ends.

Babette's Feast

Ciné Lumière

South Kensington underground station spits me back up to the surface of London between the Natural History Museum and the Victoria and Albert Museum. The underground exit here is quite elegant, but a bit dilapidated; it could do with some attention, be cleaned up a bit.

The view that greets me when I emerge from underground is spectacular. Both museums are impressive buildings in their own rights, regardless of the treasures they hold within. I admire the intricately sculpted pillars along the Henry Cole Wing of the V&A before I enter the museum, which modestly describes itself as the world's greatest museum of art and design.

The V&A is truly stunning. The marble entrance hall and staircases set the tone for this beautiful museum. I start this visit by taking a look at the 'Light from the Middle East' photography exhibition, featuring photographs by thirty artists from the Middle East. With the Arab Spring still reverberating, brutally so in Syria, this is certainly a timely exhibition.

Highlights of the exhibition include Iranian photographer Mehraneh Atashi's picture 'Bodiless I', showing the inside of a traditional Iranian wrestling gym; Abbas Kowsari's picture of a Kurdish combatant in northern Iraq wearing an incongruous Bryan Adams T-shirt; Youssef Nabil's 'The Yemeni Sailors of South Shields', a very dignified and intriguing portrait of one of the last surviving Yemeni men who settled as shipworkers in South Shields in the north of England; and Afghan writer, film director and photographer Atiq Rahimi's gripping 'On the threshold of time', a striking portrait taken in the ruins of Kabul after the fall of the Taliban in 2002.

The Jameel Gallery of Islamic Art draws me in after I view the 'Light from the Middle East' exhibition. The Islamic Art collection is amazing and I spend so long here that I don't have time to visit the Japan collection in the neighbouring Toshibe Gallery.

Instead, I wander through Room 74's '20th Century, Internationalism & Modernism' collection. There is some great stuff here. I really like the amusing sculpted head of what looks like an old Empire explorer wearing Biggles-style round glasses with bizarre orange lenses, a long thin pipe protruding from his mouth straight at the viewer rather than at the jaunty angle at which pipe smokers normally clamp their pipe.

The other exhibit that grabs my attention in this room is the 1936 painted card, perspex and wood model of Gatwick Airport Terminal. That may not sound very exciting, but the model beautifully depicts the superb art deco architectural style of the original terminal building at Gatwick airport. It is called the Beehive. In the 1950s it became obsolete and was converted into the office complex that it is today. The circular design of the original terminal, with its telescopic corridors connecting the lounges to the departing planes as well as bringing arrivals into the customs and immigration halls, is aesthetically very pleasing.

The V&A is about to close so I make a quick dash up to the 'Britain 1760-1900' collection on Level 4, where I can't help but admire the extravagant name of Yorkshire-born artist Julius Caesar Ibbetson the elder. What a name. The rest of this great museum will have to wait for a future visit.

I head out from the V&A into what seems to be a French enclave in these swish South Kensington environs. There is the French Embassy, the Lycée Français Charles de Gaulle, and the Institut Français. There is also the cinema I am going to tonight, the French Institute's Ciné Lumière on Queensberry Place.

I get slightly confused when trying to find the cinema; I thought I had found it, but what I had found on Cromwell Place was probably an administrative office for the French Institute. After pottering around for another five minutes I track down the French Institute building that I am after, the one containing Ciné Lumière where tonight's film *Babette's Feast* is showing.

This venue was inaugurated by the then President of France, Jacques Chirac. The interior of the French Institute is light, bright and airy; it makes a good impression on you when you enter. The cinema auditorium is surprisingly big, a large cavern with very comfortable blue-grey seats and a decent-sized screen. Cultural institutes normally have fairly modest-sized cinemas, if they have a cinema at all, so Ciné Lumière comes as a pleasant surprise. It probably indicates the cultural significance attached to film by the French authorities.

Savouring the extremely generous leg room provided by the seating in the auditorium, I settle back as the lights go down. Disappointingly, the pre-film adverts are the same as at the mainstream cinemas I have been to recently. Somehow I doubt that anyone in tonight's audience of mild-mannered European arthouse film aficionados is going to respond to the macho advert urging viewers to apply to become a Royal Marine Commando. That advert has missed its target audience by quite a distance here tonight.

Babette's Feast, a melancholy Danish drama, was released in 1987. It got good reviews and won awards at the time. The cast is highly respected. The script is very well written, with real literary merit. Set in the remote west coast of Jutland, the scenery has a desolate beauty that is quite moving.

But despite all its undoubted qualities, I have to file *Babette's Feast* under worthy but dull. The puritanical religious mentality of the Jutland folk in this film is stultifying; the ongoing quick exchange of glances between characters soon becomes tiresome; and the hypocrisy of the pastor father-figure who denies his daughters the possibility of finding love and getting married, yet who himself presumably was married, goes unchallenged.

The feast at the end of the film is very well filmed. I enjoy this scene, but by the time it comes around I am struggling to stay awake. *Babette's Feast* is a well made film and it just about merits the effort of sitting through it, but I don't see myself ever choosing to watch it again.

Outside after the film ends, I use a different entrance to South Kensington underground station compared to the one I used when I arrived here earlier today. This time I use the Pelham Street entrance, which has ironwork with beautiful curving flourishes between the entrance pillars in which the words 'Metropolitan and District Railways' and 'South Kensington Station' are written in what must be the original 1868 script. I linger for a while to take in this elegance before going underground.

End of Watch

Empire Leicester Square

Saturday morning sees me walking briskly along Eversholt Street past Euston train station towards Camden. I don't want to saunter around here because the street is tatty, lined with seedy dvd shops, a sauna, and a string of very downbeat cafés that do not look particularly inviting.

So I march on up to Camden, which is oozing alternative culture character today in its shops and street life. The tourists here are looking for, and finding, something edgier and rawer than the clichéd postcard London of Big Ben, the Houses of Parliament, and the London Eye.

The fashion shops on Camden High Street are an eye-popping sight: a shoe shop has a huge yellow shoe, at least three times the size of a person, sticking out from its façade, whilst the clothes store next door to it responds with an equally gargantuan dummy's legs clad in skinny black jeans. Clusters of goths and punks, locals and tourists, stallholders and shoppers are dotted around the Camden streets. You can feel a sense of freshness and energy in the air, even on this overcast January morning.

I wander up to Camden Lock and savour the great atmosphere in the adjacent market with all the old stables and the stores and stalls in the archways under the train tracks. One of the rail lines up above the market is still in use and you can still hear trains rumbling past.

I have a mulled wine at the Chalk Farm Road entrance to the Stables Market. It tastes great and is perfectly warming. Down by the bridge over the canal I admire the quirky scooter seats overlooking the canal, placed here for customers of the adjacent noodle stalls. The scooter seats look great, very distinctive.

Having spent a very enjoyable hour or so wandering around Camden, I start walking along the Regent's Canal towpath towards Kings Cross. It's a dull grey day today so everything is looking a bit drab, but you can imagine this walk being quite attractive in better weather at a warmer time of year. The towpath is not very wide. It's easy to understand why there is so much antagonism between the pedestrians and the cyclists who use this towpath to commute to and from work. It wouldn't be hard to accidentally fall in the canal, either as a pedestrian startled by a speeding cyclist or as a cyclist knocked off course by a pedestrian's flailing arm.

An old British Waterways Board sign indicates the St. Pancras Yacht Basin, a very picturesque little haven between the towpath and the railway lines serving St

Pancras train station. Some empty beer bottles are floating neck up in the water, as if they are standing to attention. An abandoned Christmas tree is stuck in the canal just a few feet before the water gushes over the lock, the tree refusing to be carried any further downstream than it already is.

It is a soothingly downbeat walk along the towpath today. Because it's a Saturday, there are no commuters so I don't need to watch out for cyclists or dodge other pedestrians; there are only a few people around at the moment.

I leave the canal at Stable Street and head over to Kings Cross station where I have a light lunch of sushi and edamame before continuing on to the Empire Leicester Square for *End of Watch*, a hugely entertaining film starring Jake Gyllenhaal and Michael Peña as two young police officers patrolling some extremely mean streets in Los Angeles. Films like this make you wonder how police forces in cities like Los Angeles manage to attract any new recruits at all, given the terrifying psychopathic drug dealers, pimps and human traffickers they have to confront on a daily basis.

The Empire Leicester Square is clean and well looked after, as you would hope for in a flagship venue such as this. Other, bigger screens in the cinema are showing *Life of Pi* and *Pitch Perfect* but judging by the trailers I don't like the look of either of those films, so I find myself in the very small Screen 8. My seat is at one end of row B. The screen is only a few feet away from me. It's a mid-afternoon showing. Not many other people are in here today.

David Ayer, the director and writer of *End of Watch*, also wrote the 2001 hit *Training Day* and he injects *End of Watch* with the same excitement and energy that animated *Training Day*. If you like one, you will probably like the other.

End of Watch is very well paced. It is very much a buddy movie focused on Gyllenhaal and Peña's characters. The story unfolds with a good mixture of action and talk, with plenty characterization rather than relying on a relentless sequence of car chases and shootouts.

Having Gyllenhaal's character enrolled in a film-making class provides a good pretext for parts of this film to be shot by the character himself, which gives a fly-on-the-wall documentary feel to some scenes. This reduces the distance between the viewer and the action and helps draw you in to the character's world. The banter between Gyllenhaal and Peña as they drive around in their patrol car also makes you like them; you see them for the good-natured, interesting individuals that they are rather than as one-dimensional action heroes.

Anna Kendrick is very good as the wife of Gyllenhaal's character. One of the most subtle moments of the film comes during the wedding reception when Peña gives a speech and instead of carefree happiness, the look that flits across Kendrick's face is one of what-have-I-got-myself-into. By marrying into the Los Angeles police, she has entered a life that will be defined by unpredictable and brutal violence, and that look on her face shows that she knows it.

At the end of the film, someone sitting in the row behind me springs up from his seat and is out the door almost before the credits start to roll. He doesn't have the desperate demeanour of someone who is dashing to the toilet. He must have places to go, people to see.

The Coal Hole pub on the Strand beckons me for a post-film beer. Built in 1903-4, the Coal Hole is an olde English revival-style pub, oozing Edwardian charm. I order a pint of Nicholson's Pale Ale. It has a great taste and goes down very smoothly. I find a stool to perch on by the window opposite the beautifully elegant wooden bar counter. This L-shaped bar has a high ceiling and an impressive frieze high up on the wall behind the bar. There is a nice laidback atmosphere in here, with mellow music playing and contented chatter amongst the gathered drinkers.

Before I leave I pay a visit to the gents toilet where a piece of graffiti saying "If ye pish, dinna flish" has been carved into a wooden surface by a presumably Scottish visitor.

Sunset Boulevard

Rio Cinema Dalston

To get to Dalston, I take the underground Victoria Line from Kings Cross to Highbury & Islington and change there for the overground line to Dalston Kingsland. At Kings Cross there is now a Harry Potter corner, complete with a dedicated bookstore and a trolley seemingly half-swallowed by the wall at the fictional Platform 9¾.

This trolley point is now set up as a photo opportunity for tourists, who can pose with the trolley and have their picture taken as they pretend to push it through the wall into Harry's magical world. A man in railway uniform is on hand to maintain an orderly queue of tourists and also to advise people as to how they should pose for their pictures.

Highbury & Islington station does not offer the same sense of a potential magical other world. Rather, it is a plain functional station serving the purpose of humdrum commuting, shopping and otherwise getting around. The signage at this station and at other stations on this line is orange-ringed instead of the more familiar red-ringed. Apparently this is deliberate branding to differentiate the London Overground with orange, whereas the London Underground uses red. But orange does not look nearly as good as the crisp red that is used for the circle on the iconic underground bullseye station signage.

At Dalston Kingsland station I get off the overground train and set off along Kingsland High Street towards the Rio Dalston cinema. It's a misty murky Sunday here in east London. Tall, slim, elegant black-painted lamp posts run along each side of the road, looking very distinctive in an austere minimalist way.

The cinema is only a few minutes walk from the station and there is still over an hour before the film is due to start, so I drop into Şömine restaurant for a quick lunch.

Situated in the ground floor of the old Dudley's department store, whose architectural grandeur is still to be admired despite having faded over the years, Şömine is one of the many Turkish restaurants in the area. I go in and take a seat and make the mistake of asking to see the menu, forgetting that in places like this you go up to the counter and pick out what you want from what you see.

The waiter is friendly and helpfully describes all the dishes that are sitting there. I choose the chicken on the bone with potatoes, and a side dish of rice. It's a great meal. The chicken is tender and delicious and the rice is extraordinarily tasty. The Efes beer is good too. Some great Turkish music is playing in the background. I have really struck lucky with this restaurant and will definitely come here again.

Well fuelled, I head for the Rio. From outside on the street the cinema looks unremarkable, a squat building on a corner site. Its exterior was far more impressive back in 1915 when it was known as the Kingsland Empire. Photos from that era show that the cinema had a tall, ornate and spectacular hexagonal tower that is sadly long gone.

However, the magic of the Rio resides not in its exterior but within its superb auditorium.

When I enter the auditorium this dull Sunday afternoon, the beautiful curves, long flowing lines, and art deco light fixtures and wall mounts of this amazing space take my breath away. The ceiling and upper walls are light blue, with red for the lower walls. With its sleek, uncluttered and perfectly balanced expression of art deco and streamline moderne design, this auditorium has a real presence in itself rather than just being a room in which films happen to be shown.

It is the most aesthetically pleasing auditorium I have been to in London; not as busily extravagant as the Phoenix in East Finchley, or as immensely imposing as Screen 1 at Odeon Leicester Square, but beautifully flowing and alive. It is the perfect setting to watch today's film, the 1950 classic *Sunset Boulevard*.

The background music playing before the film starts is Mozart's wonderful Piano Concerto No. 23.

Seats are unallocated, so I choose a seat way off at the right hand end of a middle row in the stalls. The circle does not seem to be open this afternoon, but that doesn't matter as it is good to view the beautiful curve of the circle from down below. The seat I have chosen does not give the best view of the screen – for that I could have sat more centrally – but from out here on the end of a row I get a perfect angle for viewing the splendour of the auditorium's design. Even during the film, I occasionally look up and across to admire the clean sweeping curves of this stunning design.

Cinema architect Frank Ernest Bromige designed this auditorium in 1936, and it is the only one of his cinema buildings still in use as a cinema. I feel privileged to be sitting here, and the film hasn't even started yet.

Before the film starts there is an interesting introduction from the stage by one of the organizers of the series of films in tribute to costumiers, of which *Sunset Boulevard* is a part. The speaker highlights the contribution of Edith Head, who designed the costumes for Gloria Swanson in *Sunset Boulevard* as well as for many of Swanson's other films. An appreciation of the role played by costume designers adds to the enjoyment of watching this and other films. It's good to have a pre-film introduction like this one today; it adds to the sense of occasion for the screening.

From the first few seconds of *Sunset Boulevard*, I know that this is going to be a great film. The close-up of the tarmac, the camera gliding swiftly over it before pulling back to show the boulevard, this draws the viewer in smoothly and effectively. Little time is wasted in getting to the voiceover delivered by what we know is a dead guy; this improbable challenge to our disbelief-suspending abilities sits well with the dry offbeat humour that courses through this superb film.

Writers Charles Brackett, Billy Wilder and D.M. Marshman Jr have come up with a great storyline and dialogue that is so sharp and entertaining that it keeps you hanging on every word.

William Holden as struggling screenwriter Joe Gillis, and Gloria Swanson as faded diva Norma Desmond, are both magnificent in this film. Gillis' jaunty indifference collides with Desmond's haughty prima donna persona to great effect. The bubble in which Desmond lives, wilfully ignoring the changes that have occurred in the outside world and which have condemned her to a life of obscurity instead of the Hollywood fame she used to bask in, is also inhabited by her former husband and now butler, Max, played by film director Erich von Stroheim. The oddness of this couple's existence is not lost on Gillis, who at first finds the immured existence amusing but who soon tires of it and seeks to escape from it.

The theme of *Sunset Boulevard* is the same as director Michel Hazanavicius' recent hit *The Artist*. Both films are about the tragedy of silent-era movie stars who fail to make the transition to the era of talking pictures. *Sunset Boulevard* carries extra resonance, though, through the presence in it of real stars from the silent era. Gloria Swanson and Cecil B. DeMille both made it through the silent-to-sound challenge, and there is also a very brief cameo by the legendary Buston Keaton; the one and only time I have ever heard him speak.

In his review of *Sunset Boulevard* published in 1950, the year the film came out, legendary film critic Manny Farber derided the relationship between Gillis and Desmond as shallow melodrama. But I think that is unfair, as the film explicitly comments via the voice-over that the story is about strange Hollywood folk and the weirdness of their lifestyles. Master of nuance that he was in his elaborately written film reviews, Farber gives some praise to *Sunset Boulevard* even though the overall tone of his review is less than complimentary.

To me, though, *Sunset Boulevard* is a masterpiece. The direction, the acting, the music, the dialogue, and the pacing of the film are all amazing.

As I shuffle out the auditorium at the end of the film, I hear a woman from the audience saying to the usher in a disapproving tone, "I just didn't understand – people were laughing and laughing and laughing."

I can understand her point of view, as much of the film is tragic rather than comic, but I think that the film's laconic humour simply went over her head. The script is extremely funny, in a very dry understated way; so dry and understated that for that particular filmgoer, the humour went unnoticed.

She is also exaggerating, as it is not true to say that the audience laughed and laughed and laughed. Her implication is that it was a non-stop laugh-along, whereas in reality the humour shines through at intervals rather than constantly in your face.

The tone of the dialogue is very much Raymond Chandler, hardboiled and cynical and razor sharp, though he was not involved in the writing of the script.

I loved it. I head out of the Rio feeling delighted to have seen such a great film in such a wonderful auditorium.

The Impossible

Electric Cinema Notting Hill

What a disappointment the 'Constable Gainsborough Turner and the Making of Landscape' exhibition at the Royal Academy of Arts turns out to be. There are few pictures on show from the artists whose names appear in the exhibition title. Instead, there are numerous uninteresting paintings and prints by other artists of the period who were influenced by the three headliners.

I had been hoping to see lots of works by Constable, Gainsborough and Turner in close proximity to each other so that the similarities and uniqueness of each artist and the way the three artists relate to each other would become strikingly apparent. But that doesn't happen in this tepid exhibition. The good works are few and far between.

On my way out, I notice a small exhibition wedged into a compact space on the ground floor between the gents toilet and the gallery café. Titled, 'Eros to the Ritz – 100 Years of Street Architecture', this exhibition is much more stimulating than the dud upstairs. The 'Eros to the Ritz' exhibition focuses on the architectural character of the rebuilding on Piccadilly that started in 1912. I am glad I spotted this little exhibition, as otherwise this visit today would have been a waste of time.

I leave the Royal Academy building feeling disappointed by the uninspiring 'Constable Gainsborough Turner' exhibition. It's a melancholy feeling as I think back to the excitement and buzz surrounding the David Hockney exhibition that took place here last year. Compared to that, this is such a damp squib.

I cheer myself up with a lunch of venison sausages and mash at Blackfriar pub, washed down with a pint of Nicholson's Pale Ale and a pleasingly peppery pint of Sambrook's London Winter Ale. When I pay, the receipt is signed "Thank yoo", the double 'o' in 'yoo' lending the salutation an unexpected jauntiness.

After lunch at Blackfriar I continue on to another classic London pub by nipping round the corner into Fleet Street where The Punch Tavern awaits.

Beautiful tiling on the walls, elegant mirrors and a mosaic floor in the entrance corridor signal that this is a characterful boozer. Inside, what strikes me immediately is the impressive skylight, which has a welcome effect even on this grey day, and the ornate etched panels in the bar-back. Just above these panels there is a row of carved wooden faces of what I assume is Mr Punch in a series of different facial expressions. Portraits of Mr and Mrs Punch situated high above the bar and the entrance door bookend the skylight, with both characters flanked by sculpted cherubs.

There is a nice relaxed atmosphere in here this early Monday afternoon. The friendly barmaid serves me a pint of Meantime London Lager; it is fruity and refreshing, not world-beating but a notch above the big brand mass-market lagers.

Out on Fleet Street again, I stop to admire the old Daily Telegraph building in all its art deco, Egyptian-style splendour. I particularly like the relief of twin Mercuries over the front entrance, dashing off in opposite directions, encased in a deco sunburst with 'Britain' carved between them.

In pursuit of my next beer, I go into the bizarrely named Olde Cheshire Cheese. But this pub's interior is dark and gloomy, and a slightly deathly atmosphere seems to have enveloped the small coterie of drinkers, so I head straight out again without having a drink.

I keep walking along Fleet Street as far as the Strand, where I spot a good-looking pub, The George. It has a very attractive 1898 remodelled black and white Tudor-style frontage. The George piques my curiosity by its claim on a plaque outside that Samuel Johnson used to use this place as his postal address. The idea of using a pub as a postal address is very appealing.

A further draw is that this pub offers an enticing list of guest ales.

In I go.

I order one of the guest ales, Twickenham Vanguard, a wonderful dark golden ale that slides down effortlessly. I take today's newspaper out my bag to read while I'm having the beer. One article in particular catches my attention. It is about a 'sport' I have never come across before: toe-wrestling, for which the 2013 World Championships will apparently take place at the Bentley Brook Inn in Derbyshire. This sounds like the kind of thing Chris and Tina would have included in their deranged *Sightseers* holiday.

Having finished my pint of Twickenham Vanguard, I head out of The George and up to Holborn station. From here I take the Central Line west-bound underground train to Notting Hill Gate.

Notting Hill is a great part of London. I enjoy the walk from the station along Pembridge Road and then left onto Portobello Road, which leads to Electric Cinema where today's film, *The Impossible*, is showing. After I locate the cinema I backtrack to the Earl of Lonsdale pub on Westbourne Grove for a pre-film drink.

The Earl of Lonsdale has a glorious interior. I order a pint of Samuel Smith Stout and get a warming almost liquorice glow from this dark beer as I quaff it in one of the saloon booths that ring the bar counter. These booths are fantastic – the partitions are so low that you have to bend down to get in and out of them.

There is a marvellous red-painted ceiling with plant-like flourishes, beautiful dark wood fittings, and elegant etched glass panels in the booth partitions. Three arched mirrors, each with its own fitted lamp, form a focal point in the centre of the bar serving area.

I would happily linger for a while longer in this brilliant pub, but the film is due to start in a few minutes so I return my empty pint glass to the bar counter and head up to the Electric Cinema. The auditorium at the Electric is absolutely stunning. It is a plush, luxurious, almost decadent space in which to watch a film.

I settle into one of the red leather armchairs with its own footstool and side table. Before the lights go down I admire the refined arch over the screen, the elegant chandeliers, and the beautiful walls and curved ceiling. It is a sumptuous setting.

The only thing that detracts from this elegance and sophistication is that nobody is allowed into the auditorium until just five minutes before the showing is due to start. Therefore a long queue of people waiting to get served at the bar at the back of the auditorium forms down one side of the auditorium, and most people don't get served by the time the film starts.

It is the cinema itself that has drawn me here tonight rather than the film that is showing. *The Impossible* is not a film I would have chosen to see, but I wanted to visit the famed Electric Cinema. So with low expectations for the film, here I am.

Unfortunately, the film lives down to my low expectations. It stars Ewan McGregor and Naomi

Watts as a couple who are ripped from each other and from their children by the 2004 tsunami while they are on holiday in Thailand. Before coming here, I had watched the trailer for the film and thought that it looked like a cheesy Hollywood-style melodrama, and so it proves. The manipulation of the viewers' emotions is blatant, with tear-jerking music wilfully hurled at you, particularly in the closing scenes.

The only scene in the whole film that I find genuinely moving is the one where a fellow survivor offers his mobile phone to Ewan McGregor so that he can call his relatives, even though the phone battery is rapidly depleting and might not last much longer. But apart from that one scene, *The Impossible* is clichéd mush.

As I walk back along Portobello Road after the film finishes, I ponder the irony of today. The two events I attended – the RAA exhibition in the morning and the film showing this evening – were both disappointing, but overall it has been a good day, satisfying because of the city's great pubs, streets and architecture. Heading back towards Notting Hill Gate underground station, I feel mildly envious of people lucky enough to live here in cosy romantic Notting Hill.

Skyfall

Odeon West End

The Skinners Arms pub on the corner of Judd Street and Hastings Street, just a few minutes away from Kings Cross train station, looks a good bet for lunch so in I go. From the street, this is a very good-looking pub. Old-fashioned and cosy, it has well preserved stained glass running the full length of its upper windows and above the entrance door in which the two separate glass panes each have the welcoming word 'Bar' inscribed in what looks to my untutored eye like art nouveau style script.

Inside, I order haddock and chips and a smooth and tasty pint of Brakspear Oxford Gold. I take my pint over to a seat by the window and while waiting for the food to arrive, I admire the dark red ceiling with wooden beams, the squat ice cream shaped window lamps, and the wonderfully elegant curtain rail on which the window lamps sit. Very cute miniature curtains run along the base of the windows. These curtains are only a few inches tall and complement the full size curtains that run along the higher curtain rail.

David Bowie is playing on the pub sound system. British Prime Minister David Cameron can be seen but thankfully not heard on the tv screen in the corner. I glance over at the bar counter and notice that it has got an understated but attractive slim strip of mosaic tiling running along it just below the bar counter top.

My meal arrives and the haddock is huge, so big that it hangs over the edge of my plate at both ends. I start eating it from the middle so that I can squeeze the overhanging extremities more into the middle of the plate so nothing falls off.

I will certainly pay the Skinners Arms another visit in the future for its friendly staff, cosy atmosphere, beautiful architecture and decor, and its good range of interesting beers.

From The Skinners Arms I walk west towards Marylebone. My destination is Daunt Books at 83 Marylebone High Street. The streets in Marylebone don't adhere to the strict formal grid pattern that you get in Bloomsbury, the direction from which I have come today. This gives Marylebone a meandering aspect that feels quite intimate and friendly compared to some of the other more intimidatingly grand parts of London.

It's good to wander round Marylebone and take in the bustling but relaxed feel of the area. Just along from Daunt Books on Marylebone High Street, my eye is caught by the spectacularly stylish exterior of what is now Coco Momo café bar. This was originally

The Old Rising Sun pub. A dated name panel up on the top floor of the building indicates that the Old Rising Sun pub was established here in 1866. English Heritage has made this a listed building, which is good to know, as it ensures the preservation of its striking Italianate architecture, beautiful arched windows, and the fancy decoration in what I now know are called 'spandrels'.

Though not as extravagant in design as the Old Rising Sun, Daunt Books is equally impressive, if in a more restrained, unobtrusive fashion.

As I enter the Edwardian book shop that is Daunt Books, I feel like I have entered the perfect book store. In a digital world where consumers increasingly buy books online rather than in bricks and mortar stores, Daunt Books shows how a real physical book store can survive.

It is a glorious place. It almost feels like a library more than a book store; as a book lover, I mean that as a compliment. It is a place where the physical book is cherished and respected. The skylights, stained glass windows, and the wooden floors, stairs and balustrades exude a comforting old-world feel, as if one has wandered back a century in time to a more refined and cultured era.

A peculiarity of Daunt Books is that the books are categorized by country rather than by genre. Upstairs to England, Wales, Scotland and Ireland is written on one sign so I head up the stairs and browse the books in that section. Grouping books by country rather than by genre is an interesting approach, as it leads you to chance upon books you might otherwise not have come across.

The book I buy here today is London Art Deco by Arnold Schwartzman, a great book with stunning pictures of London's art deco department stores, hotels, corporate buildings, cinemas, residential buildings, and so on.

James Daunt, the owner of Daunt Books, was appointed recently as the new managing director of national book store chain Waterstones. Industry observers are watching closely to see if he can instil the individuality and charm of his own small chain of seven book shops into the nearly three hundred Waterstones stores. Good luck to him.

There was a very minor outcry when Waterstones decided to delete the apostrophe from its original name, Waterstone's, but apart from alienating a handful of outraged apostrophe-lovers, Daunt doesn't seem to have made any missteps yet.

With my newly bought London Art Deco book tucked away in my bag, I set off from Marylebone to Leicester Square where today's film, the new James Bond outing *Skyfall*, is showing at the Odeon West End. Daniel Craig's first Bond film, *Casino Royale*, was superb but the follow-up *Quantum of Solace* was dismal, so it will be interesting to see how Craig's third Bond effort turns out.

Here at the cinema foyer, along with the other five people who have shown up twenty minutes early for this Tuesday afternoon showing of *Skyfall*, I am instructed by the ticket taker to go upstairs and wait until the auditorium is ready.

"I will tell you when it is ready", he says.

So in our small gathering of a handful of people we find ourselves temporarily parked in a holding area upstairs, a kind of limbo between but very separated from the entrance foyer and the auditorium. There appears to be a small bar off to one side but the iron shutter is resolutely down. All there is to do here to while away the minutes is to glance at the black and white photos of celebrities attending past premieres, including one shot of a very youthful-looking Charles and Diana.

The ticket taker told us he would let us know when the auditorium is ready for us to enter, but with one minute to go before the showing is due to start he still hasn't told us anything. So our little group of limbo-dwellers descends from our holding pen and enters the auditorium, where around twenty people are already sitting. We had been completely forgotten about.

Screen 2 at the Odeon West End is an impressively big auditorium, seating 832 people. It actually seats more people than Screen 1, which seats 500. It has a very good wide screen, and seating that sweeps gradually down. It is such a good-sized screen that even sitting where I am in row R, seat 43, right at the end of a row, my view is excellent, not too angular at all.

The opening scene of *Skyfall* is fantastic, the chase across the rooftops and through the bazar and the streets of Istanbul and then out onto the train where Bond and his opponent slug it out until a fellow agent accidentally shoots Bond and sends him hurtling off the train and down the viaduct the train is crossing at the time. This scene is classic James Bond.

However, that excitement is then squandered by the film makers, who clumsily insert a seemingly endless credits sequence that completely breaks the spell that has just been established. As an audience member, you feel like you are watching the credits roll at the end of the film rather than the beginning.

But with a running time of over two hours and twenty minutes, there is plenty opportunity for the film to regain its step, which it quickly does.

In *Skyfall*, Daniel Craig looks world-weary and haggard for most of the film, a Bond that is far from invincible. In fact, he looks fairly decrepit a lot of the time. I wonder how much further the film makers can show us Bond's frailties in subsequent films before he loses his credibility as heroic action-man spy.

Like Bond, Judi Dench's M character is portrayed in this film as showing her age, with question marks over her ability to still do the job at the required level. This film marks the handover of the M role from Judi Dench to Ralph Fiennes. I think that Ralph Fiennes will make a good M in future films if his performance in *Skyfall* is anything to go by. He projects an intriguing air of reliable bureaucrat with an undercurrent of shiftiness that has you constantly wondering if you can really trust him. It will be interesting to see how he grows into this role.

Javier Bardem unfortunately seems to be too nice a guy to play the villain. Bardem never exudes a sense of real menace, which means that even though you know that not all the good guys are going to get out of this one alive, the film lacks the suspense that a villain radiating evil would have provided. Instead, the villain resembles a mildly disturbed Graham Norton, cute and cuddly and camply entertaining rather than threatening.

The locations used in the film are interestingly presented. Shanghai comes across as a glitzy, high-tech, exciting metropolis. London, on the other hand, is portrayed in drab hues that seem to have disappointed some viewers but which I think give a fair and realistic picture of the city – there would be no point relying on views of Big Ben under sunny blue skies.

Likewise for the end scenes set in the Scottish Highlands; although the lonely old mansion standing proudly in its glen is a romantic cliché, the washed-out tones in which the setting is depicted gives an authentic flavour of how desolate and dull such places can be.

Another good thing about the film is the subtle way in which the familiar musical riffs that you expect in a Bond film surface intermittently rather than banging you over the head continuously. The soundtrack is much more thoughtful and better constructed than in most action movies.

All in all, *Skyfall* is great entertainment, and very enjoyable. It is not quite up to the standard of *Casino Royale*, but it is a welcome return to form after the dud that was *Quantum of Solace*.

Arbitrage

Cineworld Shaftesbury Avenue

From the 18-28 final scoreline you might assume that the Scotland versus Wales rugby match that just ended was a high-scoring thriller. Unfortunately, not so. It was a terrible game, a dismal stuttering amalgam of ineptitude that shakes your faith in rugby as a sport. Shocking to watch, it was so tedious that everyone who has just sat through it – including me – must be asking "please can I have the last two hours of my life back".

Disheartened not just by the defeat for Scotland but also by the manner of it, I summon up what remains of my will to live and head towards Cineworld on Shaftesbury Avenue.

This day has not gone particularly well so far. Maybe a decent meal will help pick things up. Just a few minutes walk from the cinema we come to Wardour Street and dive into a Vietnamese restaurant imaginatively named 'Vietnamese Restaurant'. It's a down-to-earth place and the food is good. I feel the day starting to tip in a positive direction for the first time. My prawn spring rolls are very tasty, as is the chicken satay on rice. A perfectly quaffable Halida beer takes the edge off my rugby-related malaise.

Feeling better after the Vietnamese meal, we head to Cineworld Shaftesbury Avenue. When we get here, an usher instructs us to wait in line in the foyer as the adjacent amusement arcade spews forth its unrelenting noise. When we get into Screen 7, I am impressed by the decent size of the screen and the comfortable seating.

My expectations for today's film, *Arbitrage*, are not very high. The trailer looks ok and I like Richard Gere, but I come to this film unsure whether it will have anything original or memorable about it. The film threatens to be bland and mainstream, a not particularly original tale relying overmuch on the presence of star actor Gere.

But lo and behold, *Arbitrage* turns out to be terrific.

White-haired and suitably patrician, Richard Gere is perfect in the role of a billionaire hedge fund manager whose life gets turned upside down by the death of his mistress in a car accident in which Gere's character is at the wheel. Billionaire hedge fund managers are hardly deserving of pity, and to this film's credit, we viewers are not manipulated into feeling any misplaced sympathy for a character who, beneath considerable charm, is cold, calculating and exploitative.

Although it is for Richard Gere that most people will come to see *Arbitrage*, it is writer and director Nicholas Jarecki who most effectively stamps a mark on this surprisingly good film. The pacing is just right, particularly in the first two-thirds of the film, and the background music supports the plot development in a beautifully subtle, understated way. Jarecki is a relative newcomer but on the evidence of this accomplished film, he has a glittering career ahead of him.

The other highlights of *Arbitrage* are provided by Susan Sarandon as Gere's neglected and taken-for-granted wife, and Tim Roth who delivers a wonderfully dry and droll performance as the cynical but persistent detective trying to nail Gere's character for abandoning the scene of the car accident in which his mistress died.

There is great chemistry between Gere and Roth in the first scene in which the detective interviews the businessman, the two men's mutual contempt simmering beneath a veneer of fake good humour.

The great ending to the film also helps it stand out from more predictable mainstream Hollywood fare. Avoiding the clichéd valedictory speech that had been cued up, the audience is left to fill in the ending. The jolt of this unexpectedly abrupt ending invites the viewer to reflect on what might have been said in that set-piece speech; upon such reflection, the speech would probably have delivered a smooth, manipulative and fraudulent appeal to the emotions of an eager to be duped crowd. In other words, true to the character that Gere was playing.

Outside after this surprisingly satisfying film, it's a fresh and cold London evening. It is too chilly to loiter, but we pause for a few seconds outside St Martin's Theatre to admire the amazing beautiful coloured glass above the entrance. Inside, Agatha Christie's *The Mousetrap* is playing, now in its sixtieth year.

Les Misérables

Odeon Leicester Square

Our Sunday lunch is served to us as we perch uncomfortably at the bar of a restaurant near Covent Garden. The bar here is not designed for eating at; it does not jut out at all, so there is no space beneath the bar top to tuck your legs into. This means that you have to lean forward awkwardly as you eat, otherwise there is too big a distance between your plate and your mouth into which you could accidentally drop your food.

I feel a tad aggrieved at the bright and breezy waitress who assured us that if we ordered while sitting at the bar, a table would be available for us by the time the food arrived. But the food arrives very quickly, there is still no table free, and without any apology our orders are plonked down in front of us on the bar top. The food is very good, but I won't come back here again without a table reservation, as it's not much fun trying to eat a meal with the bar staff chatting loudly to each other just inches away from your face.

The beer I have with the meal is excellent: one pint of Hackney Brewery Best Bitter, and one pint of Dark

Star Hophead, an absolutely superb golden ale that I could happily have quaffed all afternoon. But because of having to eat our meal uncomfortably perched at the bar rather than at a proper table, we decide to go elsewhere for dessert.

As today's film, *Les Misérables*, is showing at the Odeon on Leicester Square, we drop into the near-by Pompidou café for coffee and cake. What makes it worth visiting this café is the stunningly beautiful coloured glass ceiling in a flowery arts and crafts style. It is well worth dropping in for a coffee just to admire that ceiling.

Round the corner at the Odeon, the person staff-ing the box is very friendly. He exudes a warmth and good humour that you wouldn't expect to get from the often expressionless employees at big mainstream cinemas in the centre of London.

Because *Les Misérables* promises to be visually spec-tacular, we splash out on the most expensive tickets we have ever bought. The tickets cost twenty-two pounds. Each! They are for the royal circle, seats F27 and F28. It's not cheap but the auditorium is stunning and from up in the royal circle the view is fantastic, not just of the screen but also of the rest of the auditorium.

Musicals are not my thing and *Les Misérables* has already been out for several weeks without it tempting me to go see it. However, my companion saw it when it came out and highly recommends it, to such an extent that she is happy to watch it a second time. So

I suspend my apathy towards musicals as a genre and decide to give *Les Misérables* a chance.

I am glad that I do, as it turns out to be a wonderful film.

Hugh Jackman is unlucky not to have won an Oscar for his magnificent performance as the heroic Jean Valjean. In effect, he gives two performances, both of which are fantastic: first as the downtrodden prisoner with just a number not a name, and second as the respectable member of society in the new life he has forged for himself.

The bane of Valjean's existence is police official Javert, played by Russell Crowe. Crowe's singing is not up too much, and it would have been hard to sit through such a long film if there had been more of him in it. But Crowe does embody the Javert character very well, pursing Valjean with a blurred blend of professional tenacity and personal vendetta.

By far the most moving moment in the film is when Anne Hathaway as Fantine sings 'I Dreamed A Dream'. She does it beautifully. The song is passionate and profoundly sad, and as it ends you could hear a pin drop. Amazing stuff.

But it's not all tragedy of epic proportions in this riveting film. Light relief is provided quite brilliantly by Sacha Baron Cohen as the sleazy Thénardier and Helena Bonham Carter as Madame Thénardier. Their first scene is very funny and it has me laughing even several minutes after the scene has ended. The exuberant bawdiness of their characters is the perfect antidote to the dominant despair and deprivation that constitute the major part of the film.

When the film ends, I emerge from the cinema exhilarated. I had been expecting the film to drag, but it flew by. I now feel more receptive to musicals as a genre, and may increase my intake of them from my current quota of one roughly every five years.

The day ends extremely well, with drinks at The Craft Beer Co. in Leather Lane, Clerkenwell in the company of a friend from my old days teaching English in Greece. The Craft Beer Co. has got a superb range of beers and knowledgeable, friendly staff who are happy to make recommendations from their bewilderingly huge choice of craft beers. We decide to drink half pints in order to maximize the number of different beers we can get through in one session. Looking back on it, I can't remember exactly what beers we had that night, but they were all terrific. I will definitely be back.

Argo

Ritzy Picturehouse Brixton

Whirling snow and a freezing wind have got us pedestrians scurrying quickly along the Brixton streets. Although it is the middle of March, it feels more like winter than spring. Daffodils are beginning to bloom and some cherry blossom is out on the tree branches, but my fingers are numb with cold.

To escape from the icy wind, I dive into the narrow shelter of Reliance Arcade with its tiny shops on either side. The woman walking just in front of me seems to know everyone in the arcade, greeting one of the shopkeepers with a friendly, "How are you, darling? All right?"

Through Reliance Arcade and out the other end, I come to Market Row, a market arcade with a wonderfully laidback, cosmopolitan vibe.

There are several tempting eating places in the area, both within the arcades and round about. But I am here in Brixton for an early showing of *Argo* at the Ritzy cinema, so there's no time to stop for a meal. I walk past Electric Avenue, the name of which immediately evokes the Eddy Grant single from the 1980s, and on to Coldharbour Lane where the cinema stands.

The street name 'Coldharbour Lane' strikes me as slightly odd, as there doesn't seem to be any maritime feel to this area. But as I later discover, 'cold harbour' historically refers to a rough shelter for travellers along a highway, a place where there is a roof for the night but not much more.

On the opposite side of the street from the Ritzy, on the corner building that now houses a KFC, I notice an inscription that reads "Ich Dien", which is German for "I Serve". The "Ich Dien" motto is part of the badge of the Prince of Wales, which may explain its presence on a building here in Brixton. All around this area there is lots of great architecture to admire, including the Ritzy cinema itself.

It is a relief to get out of the freezing wind and into the cinema.

The Ritzy foyer and bar area has a cosy welcoming atmosphere. The cinema is of the rabbit warren variety, with corridors branching off in different directions to each screen. *Argo* is showing today in Screen 2, a good auditorium with comfy red seats.

The film lives up to expectations; it is well acted and paced, and the dialogue is crisp and entertaining. A particularly good scene is the one where Hollywood producer Lester Siegel (Alan Arkin) takes Ben Affleck's Tony Mendez character along to a meeting with Max

Klein (Richard Kind). It's a great scene, with Arkin and Kind exchanging hilariously contemptuous derogatory comments in bruising Hollywood style.

A lot of *Argo's* energy derives from the collision of the two alien cultures which the story spans: fundamentalist revolutionary Iran on the one hand, and brash superficial Hollywood on the other.

The storming of the American embassy in Teheran and the ensuing escape of six embassy staffers is gripping to watch. Ben Affleck's direction keeps things moving along with just the right mix of action and more thoughtful moments, as when the six house guests are shown helplessly contemplating their dismally limited options while holed up at the official residence of the Canadian ambassador, or when Affleck is alone in his Teheran hotel room, temporarily cocooned from the revolutionary fervor going on outside in the city.

It's always good to see John Goodman popping up in a film, and he is entertaining as ever in what is a fairly limited role. There is also an interesting, though brief, voiceover at the end of the film by the then President Jimmy Carter.

After the film I venture back out into the wintry March chill. I take the Victoria Line underground back to the city centre where I meet up with a friend at the Coach & Horses pub on Greek Street in Soho. This is a great pub, with distinctive cast iron pillars outside and an original spittoon trough inside, the latter thankfully no longer in use. After sinking a quick pint each, we move on to nearby Bincho for some great Japanese skewers and saké, followed by more drinks at a tiny Spanish bar before ending the night with a pint at The Wheatsheaf on Rathbone Place, a splendid pub redolent with history and atmosphere.

Hitchcock

Odeon Leicester Square

While walking along Upper St Martin's Lane, I spot The Cinema Store, an intriguing-looking shop which lures me in with its wide range of cinema-related books, costumes, dvds and sundry other items. I could have browsed here for an hour but time is pressing so I make do with one purchase, David Hughes' entertaining book Tales from Development Hell – The Greatest Movies Never Made?

The introductory chapter 'Welcome to Development Hell' provides a succinct exposé of the ludicrously inefficient workings of the film industry, pinpointing the conflicting forces that conspire to stymie the smooth production of a good script. The chapter on the million-dollar script *Smoke and Mirrors*, which never got made into a film despite the ever growing mass of money spent on it as well as the potential involvement at various times of Sean Connery, Michael Douglas and Catherine Zeta-Jones, is particularly revealing of the wastefulness of the Hollywood development system.

Some of the quoted comments from one of the writers hired to do one of the endless rewrites of the script are so crass and arrogant that it leads one to conclude that in the business of Hollywood writing, as in every other corporate setting, it is not the people with talent that rise to the top but rather it is the loudest, pushiest ones. That would certainly explain, at least partially, the moronic quality of many Hollywood mainstream films.

David Hughes' book is well written and funny, and it makes you wonder how any scriptwriter can maintain their sanity in the face of the ignorant and contradictory rewrite demands made by producers, studio executives, directors and actors.

Back out on the street it's typical British weather for the month of March – snow, sun, wind and rain in quick succession. It's the kind of weather that heightens your senses, and your appetite. So we dive into Souk Medina's colourful warm embrace for a very good lunch of couscous royale, lamb with prunes and saffron rice, accompanied by a mango juice and a surprisingly good non-alcoholic Chorbet cocktail.

I'm not generally a fan of non-alcoholic versions of alcoholic drinks. What's the point? But I go for the Chorbet as I am still nursing a mild hangover from yesterday when I had wine at lunch time and beer in the evening. Yesterday's lunch was at one of London's fancier restaurants, Roux at The Landau on Portland Place. We had wanted to make a reservation at chef

Michel Roux Jr's Le Gavroche, but even though I tried to book a table nearly three months in advance it was fully booked. So we tried another of Michel Roux Jr's restaurants, Roux at The Landau, and managed to get a table there in its beautiful elegant oval room, with a view of the art deco splendour of nearby BBC Broadcasting House. The meal was wonderful. Starters of scallops and quail, and mains of lamb and Gigha halibut. Washed down with one glass of Basa Blanco and one glass of Chablis. For an upmarket restaurant, the service was refreshingly friendly and down-to-earth rather than stiff and formal.

From Souk Medina we wander through occasional gusts of snow towards Odeon Leicester Square to see today's film, *Hitchcock*, starring Anthony Hopkins, Helen Mirren, and Scarlett Johansson.

It's a very good film. Anthony Hopkins is perfect as Alfred Hitchcock, the strange man-child whose genius is not enough to persuade his Hollywood studio to finance his desired production of *Psycho*. Hopkins makes the Hitchcock character witty and entertaining, moody and obstinate, blinkered and visionary. His on-screen presence is riveting throughout the whole film.

It's good to see Hitchcock portrayed not simply as a weirdo misfit, but as a married man whose professional ambitions are putting his domestic situation at risk. If the new film fails, he and his wife could lose their house.

It's not just Anthony Hopkins who is good in this film. Helen Mirren is superb as Alma Reville, Hitchcock's wife. She is a vibrant character in her own right and she gradually loses patience with being in the shadow of her illustrious husband. In one of the best scenes in the film, she puts Alfred firmly in his place when he accuses her of not giving him enough support in his film endeavours. Alfred's aloofness, compounded by his obsession with the leading ladies who appear in the films he directs, almost drive Alma out of their marriage.

Scarlett Johansson is also excellent in this film. As Janet Leigh, Johansson oozes 1950s Hollywood glamour. Even though we all know what's coming, the shower scene with Hopkins lunging at her with a knife is truly chilling. In that scene we see that Hitchcock is not the washed-up has-been that the media are portraying him as; he still has deep reserves of menace to draw upon.

Lincoln

Vue West End

The pleasure of wandering in London, particularly along the River Thames, is enhanced by seeing the London paintings of French fauvist André Derain. Derain's pictures from 1906-7 are painted in bold vibrant colours that create a refreshingly uplifting image of the city, in contrast to so many portrayals of London as a grim grey metropolis. Of course, London can be grim and grey but it can also be fabulously bright and colourful.

Derain was commissioned by his dealer Ambroise Vollard to paint fifty London scenes. The results are stunning, even though Derain produced only around thirty pictures rather than the fifty originally intended.

The extravagant use of colour is the most striking feature of Derain's London cityscapes. 'Big Ben, London' (1906-7) shows the Palace of Westminster from the Albert Embankment with the sky rendered in shimmering dashes of green paint, whilst a mosaic of light and dark orange dashes forms a solid track of sunlight reflected in the Thames; 'The Palace of Westminster' (1906-7) has a more subdued palate and a more classical feel, though still striking in its surprising colour contrasts between the river in the foreground and middle distance; and 'The Thames at Westminster Bridge' (1906-7) shows a marvellous patchwork sky beneath which Westminster Bridge is painted in green and bright pink, which sounds absurd but works very well.

'Hungerford Bridge at Charing Cross' (1906-7) is maybe the best example of Derain's spectacular use of colour in the London paintings, with red, green, purple, yellow, blue and pink jutting up against each other in a visually arresting way, as well as the divisionist style of brushwork in the lower right section of the picture which very effectively renders the effect of sunlight on the river water; 'Saint Paul's Cathedral from the Thames' (1906-7) basks in warm glowing red, orange and pink tones which give the scene an almost Mediterranean feel; and 'The Thames and Tower Bridge' (1906-7) is incredibly vibrant through its juxtaposition of green river, bright red boats, and blue bridge.

As with all great artists, Derain's pictures enable us to see familiar sights in a new and invigorating light.

Lunch in London today is at the Old Star pub at 66 Broadway, Westminster. This pub features in the Westminster and Soho segment of the Capital Cask Ale Trail, a beer lovers' route from the West End to near Buckingham Palace. My beers of choice this lunch time are Old Golden Hen and Wainwright Golden Ale, both of which slide down nicely without being particularly memorable.

Feeling reasonably mellow, after lunch I head off in the direction of Tate Modern intending to visit the 'Lichtenstein: A Retrospective' exhibition.

But it's not to be.

When I get to the Tate Modern, the queue for tickets is short but it just is not moving at all. After a few minutes I lose patience and abandon the venue without seeing the Lichtenstein exhibition. It's not an exhibition that I had been hugely excited about. I would have been interested to give it a chance, but not if it meant standing still in a stationary queue in the cavernous Tate Modern ticket desk area.

So from Tate Modern I walk back across to the other side of the Thames and have a leisurely ramble towards the Vue West End cinema on Leicester Square. On the way, a fox goes trotting along the middle of a street just off Drury Lane, turning the heads of startled pedestrians.

"It's the first time I've seen a fox in the middle of the day", says one onlooker.

Vue West End cinema in Leicester Square is showing Steven Spielberg's *Lincoln*, which by all accounts features an amazing performance by Daniel Day Lewis in the title role. My expectations are thus quite high for today's film as I settle down in Screen 4 for this evening's showing.

Lincoln lives up to its hype. It has an epic quality that will make it endure for years to come. Daniel Day Lewis is enthralling as the President stuck on the horns of a seemingly intractable dilemma – which evil to end first, the carnage of the civil war or the slavery that exists in the land? Though much of Lincoln's behaviour in this film is inspiring, and sprinkled with some humour to deflate the pomposity that always surrounds power, over everything hangs the sombre knowledge that ultimately Lincoln is going to get assassinated.

Tommy Lee Jones makes a superb contribution to this film as politician Thaddeus Stevens, an intriguing character who combines a wry misanthropy with a burning passion for social justice. It's good that Tommy Lee Jones gets a decent amount of screen time to bring Thaddeus Stevens to life as a politically astute, brave maverick who refuses to be intimidated by the brutally aggressive taunts of his political opponents.

At two and a half hours, *Lincoln* is relatively long compared to most films. But it definitely merits its generous running time. It's a great story, brilliantly told.

After the film, we head to a Japanese restaurant for some okonomiyaki. The food is good but the tables are wedged far too closely together. The woman sitting behind me is so close that every time she sits upright, I can feel her against my back and the back of my head. It's more than a little distracting.

Cloud Atlas

Curzon Mayfair

In the National Portrait Gallery shop, after visiting the wonderful Man Ray exhibition I buy the accompanying book Man Ray Portraits, as well as the autobiography Man Ray Self-Portrait. Both books are superb.

Man Ray Portraits contains many of the photographic portraits that have become defining images of the subjects: a pensive 'Marcel Duchamp, New York' (1916); an apparently suffering, forehead-gripping 'James Joyce' (1922); the bold stare of 'Arnold Schoenberg' (1923) set against a black background that intensifies Schoenberg's already severe demeanour; 'Alice B. Toklas and Gertrude Stein' (1922) in which Stein exudes power whilst Toklas almost cowers, in a room whose walls are adorned with art that is probably worth millions today; 'Georges Braque' (1922) with Braque striking a rugged Hollywood leading-man pose; 'Pablo Picasso' (1923) in which the great man gazes past the viewer with more than a hint of condescension in his dark judgemental eyes; 'Jean Cocteau' (1925) where a brooding Cocteau is seated, holding a walking stick with an art nouveau flourish handle; 'Louis Aragon and André Breton' (1924), the two surrealist poets next to each other in profile gazing off to the right with a look of mild bewilderment; a cheerily avuncular 'Erik Satie' (1924); an imperious 'Coco Chanel' (1935); and a hauntingly morose 'Juliette Gréco' (1956).

Other striking images include 'Self-Portrait' (1916), where the imprinted hand in the centre of the composition represents a play on words, the French for hand being 'main', which is pronounced similarly to the 'Man' in the photographer's name; 'Woman smoking a cigarette' (1920), a highly unusual perspective lending this picture an eyecatching quality, the woman's head like a buoy bobbing on top of a sea of curly hair; and the wonderfully sensual and melancholy 'Jacqueline' (1930).

In his autobiography Man Ray Self-Portrait, Ray proves to be an excellent writer as well as a brilliant painter and photographer. His life story is an exhilarating journey through twentieth-century art, starting with his early days in both rural and urban New York, followed by his life in Paris with intermittent jaunts south to the French Riviera living the high life, then Hollywood, then back to Paris again after the Second World War.

Ray apologizes for name-dropping but it is his encounters with cultural figures such as Pablo Picasso, Ernest Hemingway, André Breton, Henry Miller, Alberto Giacometti, Max Ernst, André Derain, Paul

Eluard, Salvador Dali and countless others that make the book so gripping.

He is also extremely perceptive about people's motivations and the way the art world works. He describes in detail his experiences with gallery owners, clients and other players. A recurring theme is his irritation with critics and clients who will acknowledge him only as a photographer but not as a painter, as if you are only allowed to be one or the other but not both.

But overall Man Ray seems content with his lot, and the lack of recognition for his painting comes across as a relatively minor feeling of weary irritation rather than an all-consuming bitterness. In the grand scheme of things he had a great life. It would take three or four films to do justice to Man Ray's life and times. If anyone ever gets round to trying it, John Turturro would get my vote to play Man Ray. I think Turturro would be perfect for that role.

Leaving the National Portrait Gallery, I walk the mile or so to Curzon Mayfair cinema to see the mid-afternoon showing of *Cloud Atlas*. It's not a film that was on my to-see list, but I haven't been to Curzon Mayfair cinema before and the film comes recommended by someone I know who has recently seen it, so I decide to give it a chance despite its daunting 172-minute length.

Before the film I enjoy a very good, crisp and refreshing Meantime Pale Ale at the cinema bar. I then head into the opulence of Screen 1, an extremely beautiful auditorium, and spend the next three hours utterly captivated by the brilliance of *Cloud Atlas*.

To achieve harmony and coherence from such a disparate set of locations and eras is a stunning achievement.

Before coming to see this film, I didn't think it would be possible for the directors to shape a satisfying film from so many different storylines and characters spread so wildly across space and time, but somehow they have done it. *Cloud Atlas* is a twenty-first century classic.

Tom Hanks and Halle Berry are both superb in the several roles that they play in the film. I have never seen Tom Hanks as good as he is in *Cloud Atlas*; he exudes a depth and gravitas that he has only hinted at in previous films. Halle Berry is equally striking in all of her incarnations. There is a great rapport between her and Tom Hanks.

The supporting cast are also firing on all cylinders, with exuberant performances by the likes of Jim Broadbent, Xun Zhou, Susan Sarandon and Hugh Grant.

Amazed and delighted by *Cloud Atlas*, I head out of the cinema and by chance my post-film wandering brings me to Ittenbari restaurant on Brewer Street where I wolf down a decent sushi set with gyoza while quaffing some very drinkable saké. The perfect meal and setting to cap a stunning film.

Shell

Institute of Contemporary Arts

Saturday morning and I'm in the Courtauld Gallery for the 'Becoming Picasso: Paris 1901' exhibition. Small but perfectly formed, like the Courtauld itself, the Picasso exhibition features eighteen paintings from 1901, Picasso's breakthrough year. He was incredibly productive that year, turning out up to three paintings per day at the peak of his creative frenzy.

The Courtauld has used its influence in the global art world to obtain loans for this 1901 exhibition from a number of prestigious galleries, including Museu Picasso Barcelona, Kunstmuseum Bern, State Hermitage Museum Saint Petersburg, Metropolitan Museum of Art New York, and the State Pushkin Museum Moscow.

Quite a lot of people are already here to visit the exhibition so we have to wait for a couple of minutes before being allowed in. But it's early enough in the day to have avoided overwhelming and distracting crowds.

Picasso seems to have embraced his destiny as artistic genius without any false modesty; no shrinking violet, his 'Self-Portrait/Yo – Picasso' (1901) oozes the arrogance of someone who knows just how good he is.

The quality of the paintings in this tightly focused exhibition is superb. The bilious green tones and unusual upward-looking perspective of 'French Can-Can' (1901) give the viewer a debauched nauseous feeling; 'The Mother' (1901) is a very moving, bleak portrayal of poverty and alienation, its pessimism attenuated by the love and togetherness of the mother and her two children, three figures clinging to each other in the face of a world that doesn't care; 'Child with a Dove' (1901) is an unusually sentimental painting for Picasso, although there is an overwhelming sadness in the scene rather than it being a celebration of childlike happiness; and a couple of brilliantly melancholic world-weary café interior scenes of troubled brooding drinkers, 'Absinthe Drinker' (1901) and 'Harlequin and Companion' (1901).

After giving the Picasso exhibition a thorough viewing, we walk the short distance to Mon Plaisir restaurant on Monmouth Street for what turns out to be a wonderful lunch. Mon Plaisir is a cosy atmospheric place and the food is great. We have onion soup and duck terrine starters, followed by lobster gratin and roasted rabbit, finishing off with lemon sponge and profiterole for dessert. An excellent bottle of Chablis accompanies this leisurely lunch. I am relieved that we have one other couple sitting between us and a bloke who is there dining on his own, who keeps butting into the couple's conversation.

Thankfully, the pleasure of the Picasso exhibition and the great lunch make up for the disappointment of today's film, a mid-afternoon ICA showing of writer and director Scott Graham's dull *Shell.*

The tedium of this film shouldn't have come as a surprise. I had already got an ominous feeling from watching the trailer. But the Scottish Highlands are my favourite part of the world, so I thought that even if the film disappoints, it would be enjoyable to see the scenery. But the film's ninety-one minutes of Highland miserabilism reduce the viewer to a state of anaemic passivity from which it takes some time afterwards to recover.

Wind blows through telegraph wires; grey clouds drift across dull skies; lives of quiet frustration play themselves out in what feels like slow motion.

The one redeeming feature is actress Chloe Pirrie, who plays the eponymous Shell. She is terrific and I'm sure she has a great career before her. But the rest of the cast are forgettable, as is the script; if the dialogue had been better written and the actors less stilted, then this might have been an interesting film. But after half an hour of it I am tempted to walk out of ICA's Screen 2 and go watch the Wales versus England rugby match that is just starting.

Years ago I regularly stormed out of cinemas in the middle of films if I didn't like what I was seeing. But apathy seems to have crept up on me; these days I tend to stay put in the hope that turgid films will miraculously blaze into life in their latter stages. That certainly doesn't happen with *Shell*, and I trudge dejectedly out the ICA cinema at the end of it.

The Great Beauty

Curzon Renoir

Russell Square underground station, opened in 1906, is aesthetically pleasing with its beautiful tiling. I like to amble slowly along the platform here after getting off a train, savouring the station's elegant design. But it does not provide the most efficient transition from the bowels of the earth up to the surface. You have to wait for a lift to shuttle you and your fellow passengers up to the light of the day. There is no escalator. There are, however, steep winding stairs leading up and out but signs discourage travellers from using these stairs, indicating that they are for emergency use only.

We are not in any particular hurry when we get off the train at Russell Square this Saturday afternoon, so we patiently wait for the lift along with everyone else rather than ascending the forbidden stairs.

Outside the station, we cross Bernard Street and walk into the Brunswick shopping centre, within which the excellent Curzon Renoir cinema is located. Our timing is perfect, as we happen upon a terrific collection of outdoor food stalls serving tasty morsels from various countries including Poland, Japan, Spain, Italy, and elsewhere.

It is late afternoon so the stalls will be closing soon, but we are in time to order some great snacks from three of the stalls. We get some terrific takoyaki from the Japanese stall, which is run by a guy from Osaka, Japan's takoyaki capital. It's good to watch the takoyaki mixture being poured into the griddle and sizzling as it solidifies in the small scooped moulds.

After wolfing down the takoyaki, we then get an absolutely delicious duck sandwich from the Polish stall. The duck is crisp and full of flavour. The sign on the stall says that you can have your choice of either red cabbage or rocket to accompany the duck, but the friendly guy serving at the stall puts in both the cabbage and the rocket for me, probably because it's nearly closing time and he doesn't need to keep any back.

The final snack we go for, at a Mediterranean stall, is a portion of very good chicken and chorizo paella served from a splendid, huge, circular pan that must be at least a metre across.

We have eaten very well, for pretty cheap prices, happily sitting out in the open air on one of the benches near the food stalls on this grey September afternoon. The takoyaki, duck sandwich, and paella have set me up perfectly for today's film, *The Great Beauty*, an Italian film written and directed by Paolo Sorrentino. In Italian, the film's title is *La Grande Bellezza*.

I arrive at the cinema just as the audience from the previous showing of *The Great Beauty* is coming out after the end of their showing. One group of three people seem to be slightly dazed and confused by what they have just seen.

"What happened to the stripper, though?" one of them asks her two companions. "She spent her money on…what?"

A different group of friends seem less confused and more impressed by the film.

"Did you enjoy the film?"

"Yes, it was wonderful. Wonderful."

The film is showing in Screen 2 of the Curzon Renoir cinema. This Saturday evening showing is well attended and the auditorium is almost full. Several spectators enter the auditorium clutching large glasses of fine wine. The clientele here clearly appreciate the finer things in life.

Seat numbers are not allocated, so I grab a seat on the back row, which gives a good view of the screen. Before the lights go down, I wonder how distracting the pillar in the middle of the room will be. But when the film starts, the pillar is not distracting at all.

Having been impressed by the sumptuous trailer for *The Great Beauty*, my expectations are high. I am delighted when the film turns out to be even better than I had expected.

In fact, *The Great Beauty* is a masterpiece.

Visually, it is ravishingly beautiful. Its rendering of Rome is quite sublime, and puts to shame Woody

Allen's postcard cliché version of the city in *To Rome with Love*. The superb music soundtrack also plays a huge role in making *The Grand Beauty* the exhilarating triumph that it is, seamlessly gliding from decadent rooftop party beats to gorgeous choral song to bitter-sweet acoustic folksiness.

This film provides a masterclass in how to integrate music into the heart of the film rather than treating the music as a mere afterthought.

The acting in *The Grand Beauty* is magnificent, by the whole cast and particularly by Toni Servillo as the ageing, suave intellectual Jeb Gambardella, who is reflecting increasingly ruefully on his life. Whilst Servillo is undoubtedly the star, the other actors who populate this film are also excellent, such as Carlo Verdone (Romano), Sabrina Ferilli (Ramona), Pamela Villoresi (Viola), Galatea Ranzi (Stefania), Carlo Buccirosso (Lello Cava).

Great scenes abound in this memorable film: journalist Gambardella interviewing a pretentious performance artist who refuses to answer his questions; the rooftop parties, oozing Roman decadence and style; the night-time scene of the acquaintance who handily owns a set of keys allowing after-hours access to palatial rooms in which the timeless sculptures and statues seem to come alive as the light falls on them before they retreat back into darkness; Gambardella walking wistfully around the city, both in daylight and at night, quiet contemplative moments to balance the exuberant party scenes; the conversations between Gambardella and his editor, witty and urbane commentaries on Italian life and culture; and Romano, who finally heeds his friend Gambardella's advice to write something original rather than putting on adaptations of established works by other authors, but who then, after a nicely understated reading accompanied by guitar, surprisingly decides to leave Rome after so many years there in order to return to his home town.

What a film *The Great Beauty* is. I emerge from the Curzon Renoir elated by what I have seen.

Classe Tous Risques

BFI Southbank

The walk across Waterloo Bridge offers my favourite view of London. In one direction you can see Big Ben and the Houses of Parliament, whilst in the other direction stands St Paul's Cathedral and a jagged high-rise skyline. Below your feet the River Thames powers along with surprising force and speed.

But on this dreich Sunday evening the weather does not favour a leisurely amble across the bridge. The rain is whipped up by a wind so fierce that I cannot control my umbrella, which is getting wrenched inside out and jerked violently by sudden gusts. So I opt to put the umbrella away and endure a brief soaking as I scurry towards the BFI Imax on the opposite side of the river from where I have come.

Only problem is, I have rolled up to the wrong cinema.

In the foyer of the BFI Imax, I spot the machine from which one can extract pre-booked tickets. I insert my credit card, only to be informed by the machine that there is no booking registered under that card number.

Bemused, I walk over to the box office counter. The person sitting there tells me that the ticket I have booked is for a film that is showing at BFI Southbank, not BFI Imax. When I booked the ticket online a few days ago, it struck me as surprising that this particular film – *Classe Tous Risques*, a slightly obscure French film noir from 1960 – should be showing on the gargantuan BFI Imax screen, a screen on which one would expect mass-market Hollywood blockbusters to be showing rather than more niche offerings.

What a great opportunity to see a slice of stylish film noir on a huge screen, I had thought. But when making the booking, somehow I thought I was on the BFI Imax website rather than the BFI Southbank website.

Though disappointed that I would not, after all, be enjoying *Classe Tous Risques* on the extravagant Imax screen, a consolation is that BFI Southbank is only five minutes walk from the Imax cinema, so back towards the river bank I go.

"I saw it yesterday. It's amazing", the BFI Southbank box office guy says to me as he hands over my ticket for the 6.30 p.m. showing of *Classe Tous Risques*.

While sitting in the foyer killing time before the film, on my phone I read a couple of chapters of the Kindle version of Kevin Murphy's wonderful book, A Year at the Movies: One Man's Filmgoing Odyssey. I love his description of how he gets into the Cannes Film Festival without a press pass, using techniques such as 'credential block' and 'mob rush'. Throughout the book, he brilliantly evokes the joys and occasional pains of filmgoing across a gloriously diverse range of settings. Murphy's writing is intelligent, funny and unpretentious; so much more readable than the patronizing showboating of the typical smug film critic.

Before *Classe Tous Risques* starts, I have time for a quick look at a small but stunning exhibition in the Atrium of film posters by Satyajit Ray, the Indian film maker who worked as a graphic designer in an advertising agency before embarking on his illustrious career in films. His posters are superb, an interesting intersection of art and commerce. The striking typography and eloquent visual images give these works an artistic quality not often found in commercial posters nowadays, but which seemed to be more prevalent a few decades ago.

From the Satyajit Ray poster exhibition in the Atrium, I wander along the corridor to Screen 1 for the 6.30 p.m. showing of French director Claude Sautet's *Classe Tous Risques.*

What a difference an auditorium makes! Sumptuous, luxurious Screen 1 here at BFI Southbank is so much more comfortable than Screen 3 where I saw *Laura* a while back.

Tasteful jazz piano plays as background music before the film starts. It's good when a venue manages to match the right music to the occasion. With little in the way of pre-film trailers or advertising, we are plunged straight into what turns out to be a very good film, if not quite the masterpiece that some commentators have made it out to be.

Compared to most gangster films, *Classe Tous Risques* possesses an extra emotional dimension through the predicament of the two young children whom the protagonist must look after. Lino Ventura plays Abel Davos, a criminal who has to flee Italy and return to his native France because the law is closing in on him in Italy.

Ventura has a granite-like presence. He is solid and unsentimental, though not callous, towards his young bewildered children. Ventura's unflinching facial expressions are those of a man who has always faced life's challenges down imperiously, but who is gradually coming to the realization that the forces conspiring against him are now in the ascendant.

Jean-Paul Belmondo as Eric Stark delivers his usual jaunty, carefree performance, beholding the world and its machinations with a wry amused detachment. Sandra Milo is also good as the angelic wife of Ventura's character, unaware of his hoodlum occupation when she married him.

The cinematography is good but not quite imaginative enough to lift it into the very best of film noir. The dialogue is sparse, minimal; moods are conveyed very effectively by the actors' posture, movements and facial expressions, all of which are laconic and robust.

The abrupt ending, in which the anti-hero's fate is tersely announced, is fitting in its directness and lack of sentimentality.

Alan Partridge: Alpha Papa

Odeon Covent Garden

Tate Britain lures me down to the riverside this morning for its 'Lowry and the Painting of Modern Life' exhibition. With its drab and unsentimental industrial settings, Lowry's art does not appeal to everyone. But I like his paintings. They are bleak and grim, no denying that, but they are also celebratory of the twentieth century northern English industrial scene. The straight, clearly defined verticals of the factory buildings and chimneys establish a coherence and tough harmony that imbue the industrial scenes with a tolerably livable sense of place.

The people that appear in Lowry's paintings tend to be faceless figures in crowds, accentuating the focus of the artist on depicting a whole society rather than lionizing individual elements within it.

When I get to the gallery just before midday it is quite busy. Annoyingly, several visitors go up to the pictures on display and stand loitering only inches away from them, blocking everyone else's view. It would have been good if the organizers had put up a rope barrier a couple of feet away from the exhibits to prevent such picture-blocking.

By darting back and forth as gaps and sightlines open up, I manage to secure reasonable views of most of the pictures.

It's a great body of work on display here. I particularly like 'The Park' (1924), a slightly unusual picture for Lowry with its open vista and soothing green and blue palette; the oppressively foreboding 'An Accident' (1926); the apocalyptic hideousness of 'Industrial Landscape, Wigan' (1925); the grey-brown dullness of 'Returning from Work' (1929); the surprising, eye-catching perspective of 'A Protest March' (1959); and my favourite picture in the exhibition, 'Going to the Match' (1953), which perfectly captures the excitement and sense of purpose that courses through football fans as they make their way to the match.

In a brilliant essay in the book that accompanies this exhibition, T.J. Clark draws attention to the geographic snobbery prevailing within England at the time of Lowry's first solo exhibition in London in 1939. Such was the disdain with which the London-based southern art elite treated the industrial, working class north of England that the gallery in London gave Lowry's 1939 exhibition the title, 'Paintings of the Midlands by L.S. Lowry'.

Salford and the other parts of Lancashire that feature in Lowry's pictures are in the north of England, not the Midlands, but the exhibition organizers at the time seemed to have felt that the reputation of the north of England was so low in the eyes of southern snobs that the exhibition would have more chance of a positive reception if Lowry's paintings were perceived to be from the allegedly more respectable Midlands.

After viewing the excellent Lowry exhibition, I wander off to explore Tate Britain's permanent exhibition. These other spaces are much less crowded than the Lowry exhibition. For a couple of sublime minutes I have the Henry Moore area all to myself; his sculptures are strange, wonderful and powerful pieces. If other visitors hadn't appeared, I could easily have stood entranced for much longer by Moore's wonderfully strong and poignant 'Family Group' (1949).

Sated by the Tate Britain, and approaching the mental daze that sets in after a certain time of gallery-gazing, I head back outside and enjoy a fresh and breezy walk along the banks of the River Thames towards the Houses of Parliament.

It's great to be out and about, wandering in London on days like this.

My next destination is Odeon Covent Garden on Shaftesbury Avenue where the 4.30 p.m. showing of *Alan Partridge: Alpha Papa* awaits me in Screen 4. At 4.25 p.m. I am sitting alone in the auditorium, wondering if this is going to be one of those very rare and somewhat creepy occasions where I am the only person in the place.

Appropriately enough for a no-friends sad bastard Alan Partridge film, I was not able to persuade anyone to come see this film with me.

But a few stragglers come in just before the film starts. I might not know who these other people are, but it's good to have them around. Much as I enjoy some periods of solitude in other situations, sitting completely alone in a cinema auditorium is too sinister for any film to be enjoyed.

I am an Alan Partridge fan, but unfortunately *Alan Partridge: Alpha Papa* is a disappointment. There are no big laughs in it, and precious few small ones either.

It's hard to pinpoint exactly why this film doesn't work. Maybe it's because the film makers felt a need to impose a tightly focused plot in order to make the leap from a half-hour tv show to a full length feature film.

But Alan Partridge doesn't need a plot; the charm of an Alan Partridge tv episode lies in its pointless vague drifting, with Alan's excruciating lack of people skills enough to sustain a hypnotic mood of low-level existential angst punctuated by a couple of big belly laughs per episode. Transforming this Seinfeldesque show-about-nothingness into a big screen action thriller just doesn't work.

Feeling deflated – my expectations had been high and I had been looking forward to guffawing uproariously with tears of laughter streaming down my face – I emerge from the auditorium out into the foyer, where I had arranged to meet one of the people I had failed to entice to watch the film with me.

I spot my friend and tell him, "You didn't miss much…"

We head out onto Shaftesbury Avenue, always a confusing web of roads to navigate in this part of central London. But we manage to reach the Princess Louise, our first pub of the evening, without wasting too much time. After a quick pint there, we continue on towards the Craft Beer Co. on Leather Lane where we spend the rest of the night happily imbibing several different blond and hoppy beers from that bar's superb range of craft beers.

It's a great way to banish the memory of this afternoon's disappointing film.

Blue Jasmine

Apollo Piccadilly Circus

Filth

Cineworld Shaftesbury Avenue

The elegance of *Blue Jasmine* and the depravity of *Filth* give each film a very different feel, though they share in common a central character suffering terribly from mental illness. Both films are well crafted, enthralling, and disturbing.

Blue Jasmine is showing at various locations in London so I choose to see it at a cinema I haven't visited before, Apollo Piccadilly Circus. Unlike at many mainstream chain cinemas, the box office person here is friendly and welcoming. It probably helps that I am here at an early showing; if it was busier then I probably wouldn't get the same treatment.

The refreshingly friendly service continues inside the Screen 1 auditorium, where I am the first person to arrive. I take my seat, centre left, mid-way back. The ticket taker, who hadn't been at the door when I came in, approaches me.

"The auditorium isn't open yet but it's ok, you can stay", she says, patting my arm.

A few minutes before the film is due to begin a bloke in a suit comes in and sits in the seat directly in front of me, even though the auditorium is empty apart from a couple sitting three rows behind me. Why couldn't he sit somewhere else? It turns out not to matter, as after only ten minutes of the film he gets up and leaves.

I struggle to explain such a quick walkout; the film has barely got going, so the bloke surely hasn't had time to be bored by it. Maybe he is in the wrong auditorium and he is in the cinema to see a different film, but in that case you would expect him to have leaped out of his seat realizing his mistake as soon as *Blue Jasmine* started rather than making a leisurely exit ten minutes later. Perhaps he, like me, was so numbed by the ridiculously interminable pre-film trailers and adverts that it took him a few minutes to register that he was sitting in the wrong auditorium.

Cate Blanchett is superb in *Blue Jasmine*. Her character is brittle, spoilt, vulnerable, and classy. It's disturbing but gripping to watch her as she makes a determined but doomed effort to rebuild her life after her husband Hal (Alec Baldwin) is imprisoned for fraud, and her glitzy Manhattanite social life disappears down the toilet.

It's a tragic tale but it's sprinkled with plenty dry humour, as in the scene where a self-pitying Jasmine laments her misfortune, particularly the indignity of having to relocate to an apartment in Brooklyn. I wonder if that line got a laugh or jeers when the film showed in Brooklyn cinemas.

The supporting cast are very good, although the film is very much centered on Cate Blanchett's Jasmine character. Alec Baldwin is convincing as Jasmine's husband Hal, the crooked financier who provides Jasmine with her immensely wealthy privileged lifestyle but who also cheats on her regularly; Sally Hawkins is terrific as Ginger, sister to Jasmine, sympathetic up to a point with Jasmine's plight but with limited patience for her sister's snooty attitude and behaviour; Andrew Dice Clay seethes with justified bitterness as Augie, Ginger's ex, still indignant at having his and Ginger's lottery win money spirited away by Hal in one of his crooked deals; and Bobby Cannavale invests his character Chili with a down-to-earth good humour and honest passion that contrasts starkly with Jasmine's snobbery and affectations.

The city of San Francisco and the surrounding areas look great in this film; it makes you want to jump on a plane and go there.

After *Blue Jasmine* there is plenty of time before my second film of the day, so I head up to the Royal Academy of Arts on Piccadilly to visit the 'Australia' exhibition that is currently showing there. It's a great exhibition, covering both indigenous and non-indigenous Australian art from around 1800 to the present day.

Some of the Aboriginal art on display is stunning, such as Munggurrawuy Yunupingu's 'Fire Story at Caledon Bay' (1963) and Mawalan Marika's 'The Milky Way' (1965), both of which are interesting examples of paintings made on eucalyptus bark. Anatjari Tjampitjinpa's 'Ceremonial Ground' (1981) canvas has a strange eye-popping effect; when I look at it, the tightly packed circles seem to gyrate. I also like the two-tone abstract design of Timmy Payungka Tjapangarti's 'Sacred Sandhills' (1972).

There are also some great works in the non-indigenous sections of the exhibition. William Westall's 'View in Sir E. Pellew's Group, Gulph of Carpentaria, Discovered by Captain Flinders, 1802' (1812) conveys the idyllic beauty of the continent; Tom Roberts' 'Allegro con brio: Bourke Street West' (1885) is a superb example of Australian impressionism, vividly evoking the excitement and bustle of late nineteenth century Melbourne; Charles Conder's 'A Holiday at Mentone' (1888) captures the dazzlingly pure light of the Australian coast, with one holidaymaker right in the centre of the frame lying stretched out on the beach whilst dressed in the suit and hat that were the conventional attire of the time; and Arthur Streeton's 'The Selector's Hut (Whelan on the Log)' (1890), the pioneering spirit embodied by the solitary figure in the foreground behind whom a vast blue sky stretches with infinite promise.

Other highlights of this exhibition include the art nouveau mysticism of Sydney Long's entrancing 'The

Spirit of the Plains' (1897), a painting that I find looks at its best when viewed from a few yards away and off to the left, somchow the painting comes alive when you view it from there; the seemingly nondescript but warmly compelling 'Moonrise' (1893) by David Davies; Margaret Preston's wonderful 'Aboriginal Landscape' (1941) and 'Flying over the Shoalhaven River' (1942); the cubist feel of Grace Cossington Smith's vibrant 'Eastern Road, Turramurra' (1926); and my favourite painting in the whole exhibition, Arthur Streeton's 'Golden Summer, Eaglemont' (1889), a magnificent landscape filled with a sense of freedom and scoured windswept beauty.

After visiting the 'Australia' exhibition I walk back along Piccadilly to the Cineworld on Shaftesbury Avenue to see *Filth*, starring James McAvoy as depraved Edinburgh detective Bruce Robertson.

Years ago when it came out I enjoyed reading Irvine Welsh's novel Filth, on which this film is based; at the time I thought that the book was very funny in a deranged way and as good as, if not better than, Welsh's blockbuster novel Trainspotting.

James McAvoy gives the performance of his career in *Filth*. His character, policeman Bruce Robertson, inspires both pity and disgust as he disintegrates morally and mentally before our eyes. Robertson throws himself with manic energy and a knowing grin into his highly charged but ultimately bleak existence as an ambitious, driven individual teetering on the verge of mental collapse.

It's hard to feel sorry for him, given how savagely he treats everyone around him; but even so, by the end of the film, pity is the dominant emotion I feel towards him.

Jamie Bell, Jim Broadbent, Shirley Henderson and Eddie Marsan, amongst others, are a strong supporting cast. One disappointment with this film, though, is that Imogen Poots (playing Robertson's police colleague and rival for promotion, Amanda Drummond) hardly features at all. Poots was very good in *Greetings from Tim Buckley*, which came out the year before, but here in *Filth* she is given almost nothing to do.

This unhinged, violent and nihilistic film won't do much for Edinburgh's reputation as a city to visit or live in; then again, it probably won't have any negative effect either on the city's standing, as the people who could be offended by the film won't be going to see it anyway.

Filth is a very good, powerful film with some funny moments to alleviate and make tolerable for the viewer the hideous mental universe inhabited by the main character.

We're the Millers

West India Quay Cineworld

The torrential, wind-driven September rain forces me to postpone my planned pre-film leisurely stroll around Docklands today, so I get off the DLR train at West India Quay station just a few minutes before the 2.40 p.m. showing of *We're the Millers* is due to start. I have travelled through this area many times on the train but this is the first time I have got off here.

I like Canary Wharf, with its waterfront bars, cafés and restaurants. Today, as the September mist atmospherically shrouds the tops of the surrounding office tower blocks, even this heartland of corporatedom seems to have soul.

This is a wet Tuesday afternoon in September and the West India Quay Cineworld is thus eerily quiet for a multiplex. I get my pre-ordered ticket from one of the machines and take the escalator up to Screen 1, a clean and comfortable auditorium with a decent-sized screen. After the disappointment of yesterday's *Alan Partridge: Alpha Papa*, I am hoping to have my spirits lifted by a different comedy, *We're the Millers*, starring Jennifer Aniston.

As was the case for the Alan Partridge film I saw a few days ago, the audience here today is very small, barely reaching double figures. But the big difference is that today, thankfully, we all have a lot to laugh about because *We're the Millers* is very funny.

It's a brilliant film, full of great lines delivered with perfect tone and timing by the cast of Jennifer Aniston, Jason Sudeikis, Emma Roberts, and Will Poulter, as well as several very good supporting actors.

I had wondered yesterday whilst watching the Alan Partridge film if part of the problem was that with such a small audience, you are not going to get those infectious waves of laughter crashing around the auditorium that you get when there is a big crowd in, and which in themselves make the film even funnier. But here at West India Quay Cineworld there are only a handful of us in the auditorium, yet we are having a great time.

Invigorated by the great entertainment of *We're the Millers*, I head back to West India Quay station to catch the train back to Bank. From there, I walk along Cheapside, past magnificent St Paul's Cathedral looming large in the early evening dusk, and on along Fleet Street to El Vino, a terrific cosy wine bar where I meet up with a friend who works nearby. We have some great tapas, washed down with a very good bottle of white wine.

Then we head out from El Vino for some beers, dropping in first at the marvellously opulent The Old

Bank of England, where I down a very tasty pint of Fuller's London Pride. After that, we continue on to the Seven Stars on Carey Street, a lovely atmospheric olde worlde pub dating back to around 1680. You feel like you have stepped back centuries when you enter this place.

Our final port of call is Ye Olde White Horse on St Clement's Lane. The vivid red interior is a bit over the top. But the barman is friendly and doesn't mind us lingering, even though we are now the only two customers in here late on this Tuesday night.

Printed in Great Britain
by Amazon

34876084R00196